Great Books as Life-Teachers

Great Books as Life-Teachers

Studies of Character Real and Ideal

By

Newell Dwight Hillis

Author of "The Investment of Influence," "A Man's
Value to Society," etc.

"Ideas are often poor ghosts; but sometimes they are
made flesh; they breathe upon us with warm breath, they
touch us with soft responsive hands, they look at us with sad
sincere eyes, and speak to us in appealing tones; then their
presence is a power, then they shake us like a passion, and
we are drawn after them with gentle compulsion, as flame is
drawn to flame."

Chicago   New York   Toronto

Fleming H. Revell Company

New York: 158 Fifth Avenue
Chicago: 17 North Wabash Ave.
London: 21 Paternoster Square
Edinburgh: 75 Princes Street

FOREWORD

For some reason our generation has closed its text-books on ethics and morals, and opened the great poems, essays, and novels. Doubtless for thoughtful persons this fact argues, not a decline of interest in the fundamental principles of right living, but a desire to study these principles as they are made flesh and embodied in living persons. The leaders in literature have their supremacy less through the charm of a faultless style than because they discuss problems old as life itself—problems of love friendship, and passion, problems of ambition and the desire for money, office, and good name, problems of temptation and sin, problems of the soul's wreckage, and its recovery also. It is often said that literature is the greatest of the fine arts, and certainly it is of all the arts the wisest and most inspiring, serving at once as tutor, guide, and friend. In this era, when fiction is increasingly the medium of amusement and instruction, and when the great poets and essayists are becoming the prophets of a new social

Foreword

order, it seems important to remember that the great novelists are consciously or unconsciously teachers of morals, while the most fascinating essays and poems are essentially books of aspiration and spiritual culture. Lest the scope of these studies be misunderstood, it should be said that the author approaches these volumes from the viewpoint of a pastor, interested in literature as a help in the religious life, and seeking to find in these writings bread for those who are hungry, light for those who are in darkness, and life for those who walk in the shadow of death. Leaving to others the problems of literary criticism, these studies emphasize the importance of right thinking in order to right conduct and character, and the uses of great books as aids and incentives to the higher Christian life.

NEWELL DWIGHT HILLIS.

Plymouth Church, Brooklyn, N. Y.
October 25, 1899.

CONTENTS

I

The New Times, and the Poets and Essayists as Prophets of a New Era

In inorganic and material nature there is an impulse, whatever it may be, by which things unfold and work steadily toward higher excellence. It is with immense waste, it is circuitous, slow, with something of retroaction; but the unfolding of nature by this mute and latent tendency to go toward a better future, leavens the world like yeast, and develops it as well. This is the spirit of the ages, the genius of the universe. All creation is on the march. The stars are revolving. The dead crust of the earth feels the necessity of moving. The whole vegetable kingdom is moving onward and upward. The animal kingdom, too, keeps step, unconscious of the impelling cause. Man, as if he heard the music drowsily and afar off, joins the strange procession, and struggles on and upward also.

It is a strange march of creation, moving to unheard music, with unseen banners, to some great enterprise. When it shall finally encamp and hang out the banners of victory, no one knoweth but He who liveth in eternity, before whom a thousand years are but as one day, and one day as a thousand years.—HENRY WARD BEECHER.

I

THE NEW TIMES, AND THE POETS AND ES-
SAYISTS AS PROPHETS OF A NEW ERA

The pledge of the "New Times" is the
promise, "In the last days I will pour out
my spirit on all flesh." Therefore "Great
Pan" is not dead, morals are not sta-
tionary, inspiration is not ancient history,
and the Bible is not closed. Men have
been telling us that God once pitched His
tents close beside the tents of Abraham
and Moses. In those far-off days He made
friends with each sage and seer. But it is
said centuries have passed since the divine
form withdrew from the earthly scene.
And, lo, comes this divine overture! God's
wine is freshly poured. Each is to be a
new-born bard. Inspiration is to speak in
each voice, as song bubbles in the lark's
throat. Before the dullest eyes "the vision
splendid" dawns. Each day is to be deluged
with divinity. Rifts are made in the clouds,

signals are hung over the battlements, voices from the sky come and keep coming. Each man is challenged to make ready for a divine invasion. And God is not "of old," but is as new as the last apple blossom, as fresh as the last bud or babe. The divine dew is not burned off the grass. The divine light has not faded from the sky. The rustle of divine garments is still in the ear.

What God was, He is. What He did, He does. What He said, He says. It is little that of old He helped Moses, if He no longer helps men. The strength of our vineyards is not that once the sun warmed the Valentian hills. The clusters ripen because the all-maturing sun comes to-day, and keeps coming. It is much that God spake to man centuries ago, but it is more, that while He still speaks, the poets and patriots muse, and the sacred fires burn. To our generation God comes, pouring out His heart in tidal waves, making each man a sage, each youth a seer, each handmaiden a prophet of better days and higher things.

To-day men are saying God is ancient history. Gone forever the age of poetry and romance and heroism! No more

Shakespeares! No more Dantes! Genius has forsaken the temple. Hollow-eyed, she haunts the market-place. Science is cold and dead. Ours is the age of hum-drum and realism. At home the critics tell us Emerson and Lowell and Longfellow are gone, and have left no successors. Abroad men mourn for Browning, whose torch, falling, flickered out. Tennyson, rising in a heavenly chariot out of the temple of song, forgot to cast his mantle upon some waiting Elisha, but carried the divine garment into the realm beyond the clouds. In music, Wagner is dead, dust is thick upon his harp, and the new music does but re-echo the old melody. In fiction, the pessimists tell us, the rosy tints of idealism have faded out, leaving only the old gray morn. "It only remains for us," adds the art critic, "to copy the nymphs and the madonnas of old." "The age of great editors and the molding of communities has gone," echoes the journalist. "Let us be content to report the dry-as-dust facts of life."

No more eloquence in statesmanship, for Webster and Gladstone and Lincoln have passed away. No more oratory at the bar; henceforth only moldy precedents. No more passion in the pulpit, for Beecher and Brooks and Liddon and Spurgeon have no successors. No more liberty in theology, for saith some General Assembly: "In Wesley or Calvin God reached His limits. He is unequal to another Augustine. The book of theology is closed. Henceforth if any man adds unto or takes away from our Confession, let his name be taken out of our book of ecclesiastical life." No more creative work, only copying, annotating, and criticising. The divine resources, overgenerous to men of yesterday, have no full tides for all flesh to-day. Reasoning thus, pessimism proclaims exhaustion in the infinite. Conservatism becomes atheistic. God is bound up in manuscripts, as Lazarus was wrapped in grave-clothes. But God is a seed, not a dying leaf. God is a rosy dawn, not a falling star. God is a flaming sun, not the astronomy that describes it. God is a living voice, not the creed that explains Him. God is flaming, eternal truth, not the manuscripts in which some sage once wrote. His outpoured spirit that began as a trickling stream is become a river "deep enough to swim in."

In a world like ours it ought not to seem strange that God hath kept His best wine of civilization until the last of the feast. Everything in nature and history proclaims this as His working principle. Science tells us that our earth, now waving with harvests from Maine to Oregon, began its history as cold, dead rock. Slowly the scant soil grew deep. Huge billows of fire melted down the granite peaks; the glaciers ground down the bowlders; the summers and winters pulverized rock into soil that was shallow and poor. And when the scant plant life began, it carried forward this enriching work; the bush shook down its leaves, the tree gave its trunk to decay, the clouds gave rain, the snows gave their gases, until at last the soil became rich and deep, and earth was all glorious with fields and forests. And the animal life, too, began at nothing and increased in kind and dignity. After the snail that crawled came the bird that flew, the beast that walked, the deer that ran. Last of all came man, lord over all. Society also has moved from the little to the large, and the poor to the rich. Slowly man's hut journeyed toward the house, his forked stick toward the steam plow, his blundering speech toward the orator's eloquence, the whistler's notes toward the deep-toned organ, the smoking altars toward the glorious temple, the reign of force toward the rule of right. So slow has the upward movement been, that man must needs protect himself against pessimism by remembering that with God "a thousand years are as one day."

The individual life also re-emphasizes this principle. The youth begins indeed with rushing tides of hope and inspiration, but moving on toward his maturity the freshness and innocence of his earlier days do not die out, but the morning splendor strengthens into the richer, fuller noon. Surveying history, the scholar sees that the centuries have not been growing darker, drearier, and worse. Man's march has been upward and forward until our earth is all afire with a glory that burns brighter and brighter. Society is not like Wordsworth's child that came "trailing clouds of glory" that died out into the light of common day.

The Prophets of a New Era

Man did not begin with a great storehouse filled with treasure. Mankind began with scant resources, and slowly moved on toward these days, when society's granaries are well-nigh overflowing. Each new era brings new inspirations. God's method always is to surprise men by bringing forth the best wine at the last of the feast. Each new century wins so many new tools, arts and industries that in contrast the preceding one seems like an age of darkness, even as the sun makes the electric light cast a shadow.

Since God hath pledged to society new leaders for new emergencies, what are the signs of their coming? What go we out to see? If we ask history to instruct us, we shall see that every prophet foretelling new times has had three characteristics. He is a seer and sees clearly. He is a great heart and feels deeply. He is a hero and dares valiantly. But vision-power is the first and last gift. That vision and outlook God has given to every Moses and Elijah, to every John and Paul, and with instant skill they have laid the finger upon the diseased spot in the social life. But it is not enough that the seer has the vision that sees. Zola can describe, Balzac can picture, James can photograph deeds and traits. But these shed no tears. They feel no heartache. They paint, but do not pity. With solemn pageantry of words Gibbon caused the Roman centuries to pass before each reader. The mind of this great historian worked with the precision of a logic engine—cold, smooth, and faultless. But Carlyle's eloquence is logic set on fire. What his mind saw his heart also felt. All the woe, and pathos, and tragedy of the French Revolution swept in billows over him, and broke his heart. Gibbon worked in cold, white light. Carlyle dipped his pen in his heart's blood. Therefore Carlyle's history is a seething fire. But Gibbon's is only the picture of a fire— mere canvas and paint.

Moreover, the prophet who is guided of God adds to the great mind and the sympathetic heart a third quality. Every Paul and John, every Savonarola and Luther, has had a consuming passion for righteousness. Purity has been the crowning quality of all the epoch-making men. For lack of righteousness Bacon lost his leader-

ship.   While his head was in the clouds
his feet were in the mire.   So great was
Goethe's genius that he sometimes seems
like one driving steeds of the sun, but
self-indulgence took off his chariot wheels.
Therefore the German poet has never been
to his century all that Milton was to
his age.   During his life Goethe always
kept two friends busy—the one weaving
laurels for his brow, the other cleaning mud
from his garments.   But Paul, striding the
earth like a moral Colossus, braving kings,
daring armies, toppling down thrones, setting nations free, has dwelt apart from
iniquity.   John and Paul, Hampden and
Pym, seem like white clouds floating above
the sloughs from which they rise.   Great
was the intellectual genius of Moses and
Paul!   Wondrous, too, their sympathy for
human woe and pain!   But their supremacy
was chiefly moral genius.   In them reason
and affection dwelt close beside conscience,
and were bound up in one powerful personality, as light and heat are twisted together
in each beam of the all-maturing sun.
Heaven's most precious gift to earth is "the
soul of a man actually sent down from the

skies with a God's-message to us"; and
these are his credentials: vision-power, sympathy, sincerity, and zeal for righteousness.*

Now, if these are indeed the signs of the
prophets, then of a truth hath God sent seers
unto our age and land.   Consciously or unconsciously, the divine tides have been poured
out upon our authors.   Our writers are becoming prophets. A new spirit like a summer
atmosphere is sweetening all our literature.
In reading the works of Cicero or Seneca one
must glean and glean for single humanitarian
sentiments.   Their writings are exquisite in
form and polished like statues, but they are
without heart or humanity.   Even English
literature, from Fielding and Smollet down
to Pope and Dryden, teems with scorn and
sneers for the uneducated poor. The works
of Sidney Smith are filled with contemptuous allusions to the vulgar herd.

Until recently the English poets purged
their pages of all peasants, and the novelists
will have for hero no man less than a squire,
and deal chiefly with lords and ladies.   But
to-day the people, with their woes and

*Carlyle's Heroes and Hero-Worship, page 274.

griefs, have found a standing in literature. A new spirit has been "poured out." The new era began with "Uncle Tom's Cabin," when a slave stood forth as a candidate for hero-worship. Then Dickens became the knight errant of each "Oliver Twist," and society began to hear "the bitter cry of the children." All literature has become permeated with sympathy for the under classes. Great authors no longer look with derision upon those underneath them, and none dare insult "the common people."* A host of writers like Victor Hugo and George Eliot and Charles Kingsley and Walter Besant have come in to give their whole souls to softening the lot of humanity. To-day all literature is working for the once despised and unbefriended classes. Moreover, books that have no enthusiasm for humanity are speedily sent to the garret. Society cares less and less for work of artistic finish and more and more for books filled with sympathy and enthusiasm for man. In modern literature the books that give promise of abiding are those that preach the

* In another generation, the expression "the common people" will give place to "the people."

gospel of humanity to the poor. Verily, our authors have become prophets!

Our greatest thinkers also, like Ruskin and Carlyle, Emerson and Lowell, Browning and Tennyson, have ceased to be poets and essayists, and have become seers. A divine something is making each lyre sacred. Our singers are giving themselves to lifting up those "fugitive ideals" the pursuit of which makes man's progress. God has always stayed the ages upon some bard or singer, and breathed His purposes and providences through parables and poems. And in our day He has caused Emerson to stand forth a veritable prophet, telling each individual that being is better than seeing; telling the orator and publicist that it is good for a man to have a hearing, but better for him to deserve the hearing; telling the reformer that the single man, who indomitably plants himself upon his divine instincts and there abides, will find the whole world coming around to him. And Carlyle also was God's prophet—a seer stormy indeed and impetuous, with a great hatred for lies and laziness, and a mighty passion for truth and work; lashing our shams and hypocrisies; telling our materialistic age that it was going straight to the devil, and by a vulgar road at that; pointing out the abyss into which luxury and licentiousness have always plunged. Like Elijah of old, Carlyle loved righteousness, hated cant, and did ever plead for justice, and mercy, and truth. If his every sentence was laden with intellect, it was still more heavily laden with character. To the great Scotchman God gave the prophet's vision and the seer's sympathy and scepter.

Even our greatest art critic also has become a prophet. By acclamation we vote Ruskin the first prose writer of his century. But he has his fame because of his work as a social reformer, rather than as an art critic. The heart of Ruskin's message is: life without industry is guilt; that industry without art is brutality; that men cannot eat stone nor drink steam; that the apples of Sodom and the grapes of Gomorrah, the daintiest of ashes and the nectar of asps will feed no man's strength; that the making of self-sufficing men is a business worthy the ambition of cities and states; that ten-talent men returning to give an account of their stewardship can never thrust gold into God's hands; that man lives not alone by tending cattle and tending corn, but by the manna of God's wondrous words and works; that justice and truth and love alone are able to turn this desert earth into the garden of God until all the valleys are covered with vineyards and the shouts of the happy multitudes ring around the wine-press and the well.

Here is Lowell, also, telling us that upon the open volume of the world, with a pen of sunshine and destroying fire, the inspired present is even now writing the annals of God, and that while "the old Sinai, silent now, is only a common mountain, stared at by elegant tourists and crawled over by hammering geologists," there are tables of a new law among the factories and cities, where in this wilderness of sin each leader is a prophet of a new social order, and where

New occasions teach new duties; time makes ancient
    good uncouth;
They must upward still, and onward, who would keep
    abreast of truth.
Lo, before us gleam her campfires! We ourselves
    must pilgrims be;

The Prophets of a New Era

Launch our Mayflower and steer boldly through the
   desperate winter's sea,
Nor attempt the future's portal with the past's blood
   rusted key.

If now we examine the tendency of invention and the mechanical arts, we shall find
that even tools have become evangelists and
machines prophets of a new day. From
every quarter come voices foretelling an
age of wealth, and happiness, and comfort.
Many feel that we are upon the threshold
of new and wondrous mechanical discoveries. Already science has fashioned sixty
steel slaves for every family. Edison thinks
the time is rapidly approaching when this
number is to be increased to two hundred.
But each tool is ordained of God for the
reinforcement of manhood. Every time a
river is enslaved a thousand men are set
free. Every time an iron wheel is mastered
a thousand human muscles are emancipated.
In nature God's machines are called natural
laws. Man's natural laws are his machines.
And while the new conveniences have
brought an increase of happiness and comfort to the rich, they have done a thousand-
fold more for the poor. There never has
been an age when the rich could not travel

rapidly. But steam enables the poorest man to travel rapidly.

Always the rich could wear warm garments, but the looms gives soft raiment to the poor. Always the rich could buy books. In the tenth century the Countess of Anjou gave two hundred sheep, one load of wheat, one load of rye, and one load of millet for a volume of sermons written by a German monk. Now our people buy the works of our greatest essayists, novelists, and poets for one penny, or two. The new printing presses have placed all the classics within the reach of the poorest. Chiefly is invention refining the multitude through the diffusion of the beautiful. The time was when only the prince could afford a painting. Now photography multiplies "the masters," and during the long winter evenings, while the tired body rests, the illustrated paper causes the pyramids and temples and palaces and mountains and rivers of the earth to pass before the fascinated eye and mind. The sense of beauty once condensed in painting or statue or cathedral is now diffused. It is sprinkled upon the floor; it hangs upon the walls; it adorns the tables; it enriches the chambers of affection; it refines and sweetens the universal life.

Indeed, the workingman of to-day enjoys comforts that were the despair of barons and princes of three hundred years ago. And each new discovery seems not so much to bring power to the strong and rich as to toil in the interests of the weak and helpless. As in the olden days Jesus Christ approved Himself by preaching the gospel to the poor, so now every convenience comes in, having this divine sanction. The poems of to-day are ships and engines and reapers. Tools free the mind for books, free the taste and imagination for beauty, free the affection for social service. Thereby comes the day of universal happiness and civilization of which the poet dreams, toward which the philanthropist works. As once the prophets so now God is baptizing inventors and their tools with the spirit of service. Some Watt, perhaps, with a new method of transit, making it possible for the dwellers in tenements to journey into the country ten miles in ten minutes for half as many pence, will, through sunshine and fresh air, cleanse and gospelize the cellars and garrets of our slum districts. Soon tools are to become evangelists of the higher life.

It ought to go without saying that the preachers are prophets divine. It would be sad indeed if they, instead of being seers and living forces, should fade into emblematic figures at christenings, weddings, and funerals, or become mere guardians of theological dogmas. History tells us every new era has been created by a preacher. Guizot insists that Paul did more for liberty and free institutions than any man who ever stood on Western soil. Froude says it was not the scholar Erasmus, but the preacher Luther, who created the Reformation. It was a prophet of Florence that turned the city of art into the city of God. Those moral teachers named Cædmon, Bede, Bunyan, and the translators of King James's version of the Bible opened up for us the springs of English literature.

Cromwell's letters tell us that the Puritan preachers destroyed the divine rights of kings, that citadel of falsehood and cruelty and crime. It was Robertson of Brighton that first said that man was never justified by faith until faith had made man just. It was a preacher, Barnett, who went to live in Whitechapel Road, and in that wilderness of ignorance and misery founded a social settlement to which came students from Oxford and Cambridge to give themselves to the poor. It was a preacher, Henry Ward Beecher, who, when men said that evolution would destroy the Bible, drove out fear and doubt, and showed us that the theory of theistic evolution insured the immortality of the Bible and the permanency of Christianity.

The scholar returns from his survey, having seen that in every realm God is causing life to expand and take on increasing breadth and richness. Man's religion, therefore, is assuming new proportions, greater reasonableness, and higher ideals of service. For the church also, a new era has dawned. As our age journeys away from Bacon's theft, but gladly carries forward his philosophy; as society has left behind the sins of Robert Burns, but joyfully carries forward his sweet songs; so the church is journeying away from the falsities of mediævalism, but carries forward the sweetness and light of Jesus Christ. Gone forever the hideous dogmas that tortured our fathers! Gone forever the scholasticisms that confused Satan with God! Never again will the cross mean pacifying the wrath of an angry deity. Never again will a man be asked to debase his reason in order to exalt his heart. The church is exchanging the worship of the past for the heritage of the present, the old philosophies for the new living Christ. We have already seen the shapes of mental and moral beauty increase in number; we have seen our youth journeying toward the schoolhouse; our homes growing beautiful and happy; our workers moving in the morning hours toward shop and store, carrying in their hands the emblems of knowledge; new and nobler forms of literature coming from the rapid press, and now it is given us to behold Christianity moving forward with increasing breadth, and having the might and majesty of a river of God.

Already that divine teacher, Christ, hath touched poverty and clothed it with power; hath touched marriage and surrounded it with romance and love; hath touched the soldier and turned him into a hero and patriot. And now He is here to touch work

and wages, making them sacraments of
human fellowship. Christ is also here to
enrich each life with new and impressive
forms of mental and moral beauty. He
offers man new powers and new impulses.
The force of the ship is in the trade
wind that sweeps it on, and the joy of the
sailor is in the harbor toward which he moves.
Not otherwise the dignity and majesty of
life are in the divine motives that sweep the
soul upward and in the sublime destiny toward which the soul moves. In days gone
by this divine Teacher put justice into law,
ethics into politics, love into religion, and
planted immortal hopes upon our graves.
Having girded the heroes of old for their
tasks, He steps into the new era, to continue
the line of prophets and heroes. He offers
to make apostolic succession a sublime fact.
He bids each youth stand in the line of
heroes and seers, with Paul and Socrates and
Savonarola; with Hampden, Washington
and Lincoln. He bids each maiden strike
hands of noble friendship with Augusta Stanley and Florence Nightingale and Frances
Willard. He bids the patriot of to-day emulate and surpass the heroes of yesterday.

II

John Ruskin's "Seven Lamps of Architecture" as Interpreters of the Seven Laws of Life—A Study of the Principles of Character Building

I know well the common censure by which objections to such futilities of so-called education are met by the men who have been ruined by them—the common plea that anything does to "exercise the mind upon." It is an utterly false one. The human soul, in youth, is *not* a machine of which you can polish the cogs with any kelp or brick-dust near at hand; and, having got it into working order, and good, empty, and oiled serviceableness, start your immortal locomotive at twenty-five years old, or thirty, express from the Strait Gate, on the Narrow Road. The whole period of youth is one essentially of formation, edification, instruction—I use the words with their weight in them—in taking of stores; establishment in vital habits, hopes, and faiths. There is not an hour of it but is trembling with destinies—not a moment of which, once past, the appointed work can ever be done again, or the neglected blow struck on the cold iron. Take your vase of Venice glass out of the furnace, and strew chaff over it in its transparent heat, and recover *that* to its clearness and rubied glory when the north wind has blown upon it; but do not think to strew chaff over the child fresh from God's presence, and to bring the heavenly colors back to him—at least in this world.—*Modern Painters, Vol. III, p. 430.*

II

JOHN RUSKIN'S "SEVEN LAMPS OF ARCHI-
TECTURE" AS INTERPRETERS OF THE
SEVEN LAWS OF LIFE—A STUDY OF THE
PRINCIPLES OF CHARACTER BUILDING

Among the heroic souls who have sought
to recover the lost paradise and recapture
the glory of an undefiled and blessed world
stands John Ruskin, oft an apostle of gentle
words that heal like medicines, and sometimes a prophet of Elijah-like sternness and
grandeur, consuming man's sins with words
of flame. "There is nothing going on
among us," wrote Carlyle to Emerson, "as
notable as those fierce lightning bolts Ruskin is copiously and desperately pouring into
the black world of anarchy around him.
No other man has in him the divine rage
against iniquity, falsity, and baseness that
Ruskin has, and every man ought to have."
Full fifty years have passed since this glorious youth entered the arena, his face glow-

ing with hope, the heroic flame of the martyrs burning within his breast, his message a plea for a return to the simplicities of virtue. During all these years he has been pouring forth prose of a purity and beauty that have never been surpassed. Over against the brocaded pages of Gibbon and the pomposity of Dr. Johnson's style stands Ruskin's prose, every page embodied simplicity, every sentence clear as a cube of solid sunshine. Effects that Keats produced only through the music and magic of verse, John Ruskin has easily achieved through the plainness of prose. What Leigh Hunt said of Shelley we may say of Ruskin—he needs only the green sod beneath his feet to make him a kind of human lark, pouring forth songs of unearthly sweetness.

But if the critics vote him by acclamation the first prose writer of the century, it must be remembered that his fame does not rest upon his skill as a literary artist. An apostle of beauty and truth, indeed, Ruskin is primarily an apostle of righteousness. Unlike Burns and Byron, Shelley and Goethe, no passion ever poisoned his purposes and no vice ever disturbed the working of his genius. What he taught in theory he first was in character and did in practice. Rich with great wealth, inherited and acquired, he refused interest upon his loans, and having begun with giving away his income, he ended by giving away much of his capital. Unlike that rich young man who went away from Christ sorrowful, John Ruskin gladly forsook all his possessions to follow Jesus. The child of leisure, he chose to earn to-morrow's bread by to-day's labor and toil.

Going every whither seeking for pictures and marbles that represented ideal beauty, he used these art treasures not so much for enriching his own life and happiness as for diffusing the beautiful and furnishing models to laborers who worked in iron, steel, and stone. If other rich men have given money to found workingmen's clubs, Ruskin gave himself also, and lent the toilers independence and self-reliance. It is said that through his favorite pupil, Arnold Toynbee, he developed the germ of the social settlements. But his fame rests neither upon his work as an art critic, nor his skill as a prose author, nor his work as a social reformer; it rests rather upon his unceasing emphasis of individual worth as the secret of happiness and progress. If Mazzini preached the gospel of social rights, and Carlyle the gospel of honest work, and Matthew Arnold the gospel of culture, and Emerson the gospel of sanity and optimism, John Ruskin's message, repeated in a thousand forms, is one message—never altered and never retreated from—goodness is more than gold, and character outweighs intellect. Because he stood for a fine, high, heroic regimen, he conquered confidence, and has his place among the immortals.

If we search out the fascination of Ruskin's later works, we shall find the secret in their intense humanity. Loving nature, Ruskin's earliest, latest, deepest enthusiasm was for man. With eager and passionate delight, in "Modern Painters" he sets forth the claim of rock and wave, of herb and shrub, upon man's higher life. But the white clouds, the perfumed winds, the valleys covered with tended corn and cattle, the mountains robed in pine as with the garments of God, seemed as nothing compared to man, who goes weeping, laughing, loving, through his pathetic career. One morning, crossing the field toward Matterhorn, he met a suffering peasant, and in that hour the mountain became as nothing in the presence of his brother man. In all his later books, therefore, he is a light-bearer, seeking to guide men into happiness and virtue. He reminds the weary king and the tormented slave alike that the secrets of happiness are in "drawing hard breath over chisel, or spade, or plow, in watching the corn grow and the blossom set, and, after toil, in reading, thinking, in hoping and praying." Would any man be strong, let him work; or wise, let him observe and think; or happy, let him help; or influential, let him sacrifice and serve. Does some youth deny beauty to the eye, books to the mind, and friendship to the heart, that he may gather gold and daily eat stalled ox in a palace? This youth is a prince who hath voluntarily entered a dungeon to spend his time gathering the rotting straw from the damp stones to twist it into a filthy wreath for his forehead. Does some Samson of industry use his superior wisdom to gather into his hands all the lines of some branch

of trade while others starve? He is like
unto a wrecker, who lures some good ship
upon the rocks that he may clothe himself
with garments and possess purses unwrapped
from the bodies of brave men slain by deceit.
Wealth, he asserts, is like any other natural
power in nature—divine if divinely used.
In the hands of a miserly man wealth is
clogged by selfishness and becomes like
rivers that "overwhelm the plains, poison-
ing the winds, their breath pestilence, their
work famine," while honest and benevolent
wealth is like those rivers that pass softly
from field to field, moistening the soil, puri-
fying the air, giving food to man and beast,
bearing up fleets of war and peace.

For John Ruskin the modern Pharisee was
the man who prayed, "God, I thank thee
that I am not as other men are; I feast
seven days a week, while I have made other
men fast." And against every form of
selfishness and injustice he toiled, ever seeking to overthrow the kingdoms of Mammon
and Belial, laboring to make his land a
"land of royal thrones for kings, a sceptered
isle for all the world, a realm of light, a
center of peace, a mistress of arts, a faithful

guardian of great memories in the midst of irreverence and ephemeral visions." But from the first volume of "Modern Painters" to the last pages of the "Præterita" his one message is, Doing is better than seeming, giving is better than getting, and stooping to serve better than climbing toward the throne to wear an outer crown and scepter.

Over against these books dealing with man's ambitions, strifes, defeats, and sins stands Ruskin's "Lamps of Architecture," a book written at an hour when the sense of life's sins, sorrows, and wrongs swept through his heart with the might of a destroying storm. In that hour when the pen dropped from his hand and hope departed from his heart, one problem distracted his mind by day and disturbed his sleep by night—"Why is the fruit shaken to the earth before its ripeness, the glowing life and the goodly purpose dissolved away in sudden death, the words half spoken chilled upon the lips touched into clay forever, the whole majesty of humanity raised to its fullness, with every gift and power necessary for a given purpose at a given moment centered in one man, and all this perfected

blessing permitted to be refused, perverted,
crushed, and cast aside by those who need
it most—the city which is *not* set upon a
hill, the candle that giveth light to none
enthroned in the candlestick?" The world's
ingratitude to its best men rested like a
black cloud upon his spirit. In that hour
when the iron entered his soul and ingratitude blighted the blossoms of the heart,
Ruskin turned from the baseness of man to
the white statue that lifts no mailed hand
to strike, and exchanged the coarse curses
of the market-place for the sacred silence of
the cathedral. He knew that if wholesome
labor wearies at first, afterward it lends
pleasure; that if the frosty air now chills
the peasant's cheek, afterward it will make
his blood the warmer. But he also knew
that "labor may be carried to a point of
utter exhaustion from which there is no
recovery; that cold passing to a certain
point will cause the arm to molder in its
socket," and that heart-sickness through
ingratitude may cause the soul to lose its
life forever.

Leaving behind the tumult of the street
and the din of the market-place, he entered

the cathedral, hoping in its silence and peace to find healing for life's hurts. Standing beneath the vast dome, in vision hour he saw Von Rile or Angelo stretching out hands upon the stones of the field and rearing them into some awful pile with vast springing arches and intrepid pinnacles that go leaping toward Him whose home is above the clouds and beyond them. He saw walls all glorious with lustrous beauty, and knew that artists had taken the flower girls from the streets and turned them into angels for the ceiling; had taken the shrunken beggar, hobbling homeward, and made him to reappear upon the canvas as an Apollo of beauty. He saw chapels once the scene of rubbish, plaster, and litter become chapels of peace, glowing with angels and prophets and sibyls. One day, crossing the square of Venice, he saw St. Mark's rising like a vision out of the ground, its front one vast forest of clustered pillars of white and gold and rose, upon which rested domes glorious enough to have been let down from heaven; a pile made partly of mother-of-pearl, partly of opal, partly of marble, every tower surmounted by a golden cross flinging wide its

arms to uplift the world, every niche holding some angel upon whose lips trembled
words of mercy and healing. Lingering
there, slowly the fever passed from his heart
and the fret from his mind. Studying the
laws by which foundations were made firm,
by which towers were made secure and
domes perfect, he completed a volume in
which he forgot man, and remembered only
the problems of stone and steel and wood;
and yet as we analyze these chapters we find
that these seven lamps of architecture are in
reality the seven laws of life and happiness.
For the soul is a temple more majestic than
any cathedral—a temple in which principles
are foundation stones, and habits are columns and pillars, and faculties are master
builders, every thought driving a nail and
every deed weakening or making strong
some timber, every holy aspiration lending
beauty to the ceiling, as every unclean
thing lends defilement—the whole standing
forth at last builded either of passions,
worthless as wood, hay, and stubble, or
builded of thoughts and purposes more precious than gold and flashing gems.

Lingering long in the cities of Italy, Ruskin found some temples in the full pride of their strength and the perfection of their beauty, having passed unharmed through the snows of a thousand winters and the storms of a thousand summers. But other temples he found that were mere shells of their former loveliness, bare skeletons of pierced walls, here a tower and there an arch. Studying these deserted temples through which the sea wind moaned and murmured, and the ruins that time was plowing into dust, he discovered that no robber's hand had wrought this ruin, that no fire had consumed the arch or overthrown the column. In Venice the roof of the great church had fallen because the architect had put lying stones in the foundation. In Verona the people had deserted the cathedral because the architect had built columns of plaster and painted them to look like veined marble, forgetting that time would soon expose the ugly, naked lie. One day, entering a church in a heavy rainstorm, he found buckets placed to catch the rain that was dripping from the priceless frescoes of Tintoretto because a builder had put lying tiles upon the roof. He saw ships cast upon the rocks because some smith had put a lying link in the anchor's cable. He saw the members of a household burning up with a fatal fever because the plumber had used lying lead in the drainage. He saw the captain deceiving himself about the leaks in his boat and taking sailors forth to a certain death.

And in that hour his whole soul revolted from "the patriotic lie of the historian, the provident lie of the politician, the zealous lie of the partisan, the merciful lie of the friend, and the careless lie of each man to himself." For if untruth is fatal to the permanency of buildings, much more is it fatal to excellence in the soul. For man the beginning of lies is ruin, and the end thereof death. Therefore in John's vision of the city of God he saw there no sorcerer, no murderer, and no man "who loveth and maketh a lie." For life's deadliest enemy, and its most despicable one, is falseness. In the last analysis, untruth is inferiority and weakness. When the teacher lifts the rod, the child without other defense lifts up the lie as a shield against the blow. When the dying man asks his friends as to his condition, the strong man, conscious of his resources to make his friend victorious over death, speaks the instant truth, while the weak man, unwilling to confess his poverty of resource, tells this soft and glistening lie, "To-morrow you will be better."

In the realm of traffic, also, the wise merchant can afford to sell his goods for what they are, but the weak one feels that he must sell lying threads, lying foods, and lying drinks. But nature hates lies. She makes each law a detective. Sooner or later she runs down every falsehood. A tiny worm may pierce the heart of a young tree, and the bark may hide the secret gash. But as the days go on the rain will cut one fiber, and the heat another, and when years have passed, some time when a soft zephyr goes sighing through the forest the great tree will come crashing down. For at last nature will hunt out every hidden weakness. If the law of truth is the first law in temple-rearing and palace-building, truth is also the first law in happiness and character. When Christ pleads for the new heart, He urges man to break with him who is the father of lies and swear fidelity to Him who is the God of truth, whose ways are happiness, and whose paths are peace.

To that law of truth that firmly fixes foundations for cathedrals, Ruskin adds the law of obedience. In springing his wall the architect must plumb the stones in obedience to the law of gravity. In springing his arch he must brace it, obeying the laws of resistance. In lifting his tower he must relate it to the temple, obeying the law of proportion and symmetry; and he who disobeys one fundamental law will find great nature pulling his towers down over his head. For no architect builds as he pleases, but only as nature pleases, through laws of gravity, and stone, and steel. In the kingdom of the soul also obedience is strength and life, and disobedience is weakness and death. In the last analysis liberty is a phantom, a dream, a mere figment of the brain.

Society's greatest peril to-day is the demagogues who teach and the ignorant classes who believe that there is such a thing as liberty. The planets have no liberty; they follow their sun. The seas know no liberty; they follow the moon in tidal waves. When the river refuses to keep within its banks, it becomes a curse and a destruction. It is the stream that is restrained by its banks that turns mill-wheels for men. The clouds, too, have their beauty in that they are led forth in ranks, and columns, generaled by the night winds. And in proportion as things pass from littleness toward largeness they go toward obedience to law. Because the dead leaf obeys nothing, it flutters down from its bough, giving but tardy recognition to the law of gravity; while our great earth, covered with cities and civilization, is instantly responsive to gravity's law. Indeed, he who disobeys any law of nature flings himself athwart her wheels, to be crushed to powder. And if disobedience is destruction, obedience is liberty. Obeying the law of steam, man has an engine. Obeying the law of fire, he has warmth. Obeying the law of speech, he has eloquence. Obeying the law of sound thinking, he has leadership. Obeying the law of Christ, he has character. The stone obeys one law, gravity, and is without motion. The worm obeys two laws, and adds movement. The bird obeys three laws, and can fly as well as stand or walk. And as man increases the number of laws that he obeys, he increases in richness of nature, in wealth, and strength, and influence. Nature loves paradoxes, and this is her chiefest paradox— he who stoops to wear the yoke of law becomes the child of liberty, while he who will be free from God's law wears a ball and chain through all his years. Philosophy reached its highest fruition in Christ's principle, "Love is the fulfillment of the law."

Not less important are the laws of beauty and of sacrifice. When the marble, refusing to express an impure or wicked thought, has fulfilled the law of strength, suddenly it blossoms into the law of beauty. For beauty is no outer polish, no surface adornment. Workers in wood may veneer soft pine with thin mahogany, or hide the poverty of brick walls behind thin slabs of alabaster. But real beauty is an interior quality, striking outward and manifest upon the surface. When the sweet babe is healthy within, a soft bloom appears upon the cheek without. When ripeness enters the heart of the grape, a purple flush appears upon the surface of the cluster. Carry the rude speech of the forest child up to beauty, and it becomes the musical language of Xenophon. Carry the rude hut of a savage up to beauty, and it becomes a marble house. Carry the stumbling thought of a slave up to beauty, and it becomes the essay of Epictetus. But beauty obeys the law of sacrifice, and is very simple. The truly beautiful column stands forth a single marble shaft. The most perfect capital has one adornment, an acanthus leaf. Is Antigone or Rosalind to dress for her marriage-day? Let her wear one color—white—and one flower at her throat—a sweet briar. Does some Burns or Bryant, standing in the field of blackberries, meditate a poem, let him eat for the flavor one berry, no more. Does some youth aspire to perfect prose, let him prune away all high-sounding phrases, and instead of adorning one thought in ten glorious sentences, let him fill his ten simple sentences with ten great thoughts. Ours is a world in which the sweetest song is the simplest.

And when the vestal virgin of beauty

has adorned the temple without, it asks the artist to adorn his soul with thoughts, and worship, and aspirations. If the body lives in a marble house, the soul should revolt from building a mud hut. The law of divine beauty asks the youth to flee from unclean thoughts and vulgar purposes as from a bog or a foul slough. It bids him flee from irreverence, vanity, and selfishness as man flees from some plague-smitten village or a filthy garment. How sweet the voice of beauty that whispers, ''Seek whatsoever things are lovely, whatsoever things are true, whatsoever things are virtuous, whatsoever things are of good report.'' Having doubled the beauty of his house, having doubled the sweetness of his music, having doubled the wisdom of his book, man should also double the nobility and beauty of his life, making the soul within as glorious as a temple without.

When the palace or temple has been founded in strength and crowned with beauty, the law of remembrance comes in to bid men guard well their treasures. This building that the fathers reared out of their thoughts, their gold, their aspirations and worship, is theirs, not ours. Rather it is ours only to guard and enjoy, not to destroy or alter. Our Independence Hall, England's great abbey, Italy's St. Peter's, the Parthenon of Athens, these are not ours. They belong partly to the noble fathers who built them and partly to the generations that shall come after us. What we build we may cast down or change. But their illuminated missals and books are to be guarded in glass cases and handed forward; their immortal frescoes and statues are to be watched as we watch the crown jewels of kings; the doors of their temples are to be guarded as once men guarded the gates of the city. Profane indeed the destroying hands lifted upon some ancient marble, or picture, or bronze! Sacred forever the steps of that temple worn by the feet of Pericles, and Plato, and Socrates! Sacred the temple which passed the seven good emperors of Rome! Sacred that abbey where the parliaments of kings and churches oft did meet! Little wonder that men, worn and weary by life's fierce strife, make long pilgrimages to the Duomo in

Florence, or the great square in Venice, or to that marble hall in Milan.* Frederic Harrison thinks the Parthenon of Phidias is as sacred as the "Iliad" of Homer; Giotto's tower in Florence is as precious as the "Paradiso" of Dante; the abbey of England is as immortal as the "Hamlet" of Shakespeare. No punishment can be too severe for him who lifts a vandal's hand to destroy these treasure-houses of great souls.

And then, like a sweet voice falling from the sky, come the words: "Ye are the temple of God. This house not made with hands is eternal in the heavens." He who asks men to guard dead statues and the decaying canvas will himself guard and keep in immortal remembrance the soul temple of the dying statesman, and hero, and martyr. If Milton says that "a book is the precious lifeblood of a master spirit embalmed and treasured up on purpose for a life beyond life," and affirms that we may "as well kill a man as kill a good book," then the divine voice whispers that the soul is the precious life-temple into which three-score years and ten have swept their

* See " Sacredness of Ancient Buildings."

thoughts, and dreams, and hopes, and prayers, and tears, and committed all this treasure into the hands of that God who never slumbers and never sleeps.

Slowly the soul's temple rises. Slowly reason and conscience make beautiful the halls of imagination, the galleries of memory, the chambers of affection. When success makes the colors so bright as to dazzle, trouble comes in to soften the tints. If adversity lends gloom to some room of memory, hope enters to lighten the dark lines. For character is a structure that rises under the direction of a divine Master Builder. Full oft a divine form enters the earthly scene. Thoughts that are not man's enter his mind. Hopes that are not his, like angels, knock at his door to aid him in his work. Even death is no "Vandal." When the body hath done its work, death pulls the body down, as Tintoretto, toiling upon his ceiling, pulled down his scaffold to reveal to men a ceiling glorious with lustrous beauty. At the gateway of ancient Thebes watchmen stood to guard the wicked city. Upon the walls of bloody Babylon soldiers walked the long night through, ever keeping the towers

where tyranny dwelt. And if kings think
that dead stones and breathless timbers are
worthy of guarding, we may believe that
God doth set keepers to guard the living
city of man's soul. He gives His angels
charge over the fallen hero, the dying
mother and the sleeping child. He will
not forget His dead. Man's soul is God's
living temple. It is not kept by earthly
hands. It is eternal in the heavens

III

George Eliot's Tito, in "Romola"—A Study of the Peril of Tampering with Conscience and the Gradual Deterioration of Character

You talk of substantial good, Tito! Are faithfulness, and love, and sweet, grateful memories no good? Is it no good that we should keep our silent promises on which others build because they believe in our love and truth? Is it no good that a just life should be justly honored? Or, is it good that we should harden our hearts against all the wants and hopes of those who have depended upon us? What good can belong to men who have such souls? To talk cleverly, perhaps, and find soft couches for themselves, and live and die with their base selves as their best companions. It is only a poor sort of happiness, my Lillo, that could ever come by caring very much about our own narrow pleasures. We can only have the highest happiness, such as goes along with being a great man, by having wide thoughts, and much feeling for the rest of the world as well as ourselves; and this sort of happiness often brings so much pain with it, that we can only tell it from pain by its being what we would choose before everything else, because our souls see it is good. There are so many things wrong and difficult in the world, that no man can be great—he can hardly keep himself from wickedness — unless he gives up thinking much about pleasure or rewards, and gets strength to endure what is hard and painful.
—*Wit and Wisdom of George Eliot, p. 154.*

III

GEORGE ELIOT'S TITO, IN "ROMOLA"—A STUDY OF THE PERIL OF TAMPERING WITH CONSCIENCE AND THE GRADUAL DETERIORATION OF CHARACTER

Ever since King David's time, when Nathan used his story of the ewe lamb to indict the guilty monarch, fiction has been one of life's great teachers. He who "spake as never man spake" adopted the parable as His favorite method of instruction. After eighteen centuries, the most popular story in literature is Christ's story of the prodigal son, a story that has fascinated the generations, softened the races, and will yet win a wandering world back to its Father's side. If the Bible, with its parables, is the book best loved by men, next to it stands "Pilgrim's Progress," more widely read than any other human book. If "Les Miserables" exhibits the evolution of conscience, "Wilhelm Meister," the evolution of intellect, and "The Scarlet Letter," the evolution of 'pain and penalty, the theme of "Romola" is the evolution of sin, the peril of tampering with conscience and the gradual deterioration of character. In this volume George Eliot stands forth the historian of the soul, and tells the story of its decline and fall. At the beginning of his career the beautiful boy Tito was crowned with innocence and purity, but at last he stood forth covered with infamy and shame as with garments of pollution.

Consider the youth who enters the scene with all the promise of a coming hero and passes from our sight a full-blown villain. Early one morning a Florentine merchant, passing through a street that Dante loved, found a young Greek lying asleep in the portico of an old church. An hour later the merchant, conversing with his clerk, described the boy, with his broad, straight forehead, his youthful face infused with rich young blood, his dark, soft, velvety eyes, as needing only a myrtle wreath about his curls to make him a young Bacchus, or rather a gifted Apollo. But Tito's bright face and the richly tinted beauty that lent

his face the radiance of a sunny morning
were the least of his gifts. His, also, was an
intellect keen indeed, and wit that flashed
like a two-edged sword. His, too, the gift
of humor, and that gurgling laughter and
mirth that are contagious and make their
possessor the radiant center of every social
circle.

Fascinating indeed the history of this
youth, who made his history a tragedy.
Very early in life he was left an orphan, and
fell upon filth, beggary, and cruel wrong.
By some unknown means a traveling minstrel gained possession of the child, and
made his living from the boy's sweet voice.
Unfortunately, his master was drunken and
cruel, and oft gave the child blows and bitterness. One day when Baldassarre was
crossing the market-place he was moved by
the child's pathetic sorrow. Rescuing him
from brutal kicks, he brought Tito to a
home that seemed like paradise. Lonely
and long unloved, the father poured out
for orphaned Tito the full tides of a heart
stored with an inexhaustible treasure. Fulfilling a career of caresses and comforts,
the child's life blossomed and passed

swiftly into a youth crowned with splendid grace.

But moving along the streets of the Grecian city, the youth could never forget that some there were who once had known him as a minstrel child dwelling in want and beggary. This touched his pride. In such hours he urged his father to sell all his goods and take him to Italy, where he might pass as his benefactor's son. For even in childhood Tito was selfish. Oft had he refused his father's wishes, but refused with such charming, half-smiling, and pleading good nature that the mere pleasure of looking at him made amends to his benefactor and robbed the selfish boy's refusal of half its poison. In his selfishness it seemed as nothing to the youth that he was asking his father to leave the city of his fathers, the house where he was born, the villa with its graves upon the hillside. But the youth had set his heart upon going, and sought ever to sunder the cords that bound the man to his old home. One night, overpersuaded, the father came home to say that he had turned all his goods into the form of gold and gems, making ready for the hour when he would turn forever from his native land. One promise alone he exacted from the youth—that when death came, as come it must, Tito would bring him back to sleep beside his fathers. But scarcely had the ship that was to bear the pilgrims into Italy passed into the open sea when disaster overtook the travelers. In the excitement of the shipwreck father and son were separated. Unfortunately, the boat that saved the older man from drowning fell into the hands of pirates; while Tito, after a night of peril and clinging to a broken spar, was picked up by a vessel that landed him in Florence. Thus for a second time Providence had granted a marvelous deliverance. Having passed from a beggar's hut to a merchant's palace, the youth now exchanged drowning, or what was worse, a Turkish slave market, for that city of splendor and romance that had been the Mecca of his dreams. By two deliverances, therefore, Providence had, as it were, placed him under bonds. God had sworn Tito to a life of service, self-sacrifice, and noble generosity.

But when this buoyant youth, who had

known such romantic adventures, found himself in the city Dante loved, he fell into a grievous temptation. His bright face, easy smile, and liquid voice won friends, and swift advancement stirred high hopes in the ambitious boy. Among the events of his first week in Florence were an opportunity of teaching Greek to the sons of a rich family, an invitation to become secretary in the Scala palace, and a request to serve as librarian for a blind scholar, one Bardo de Bardi. Lest these new friends should misunderstand his buoyant spirits, he said nothing of his father's peril. In his heart he told himself that after he had sold the gems he would probably begin the search for his benefactor. But when a week had passed by, and he had kept his guilty secret, something whispered that should his new friends now discover his shameful selfish ness, they would despise him for not having gone at once to the ruler of the city to tell him that his father had been seized by pirates and was even now, under the summer sun, "toiling as a slave, hewing wood and carrying water, perhaps being smitten because he was not deft and active," and

invoke the ruler's aid to help free his benefactor. But Tito justified himself by the
thought that even if he did start forth to
visit the archipelago he might suffer a second
shipwreck or be himself seized by pirates,
and so have no means to support his father
should the old man finally be discovered.
Doubtless Baldassarre was even now dead.

Tito had indeed known of instances where
relatives had gone to crowned and mitered
heads for aid in freeing friends from the
horrors of Turkish slavery, but these were
all persons of great wealth. Perhaps, also,
Baldassarre's absence was a relief. Of late
the heavy-browed, eagle-eyed old man had
grown wearisome and exacting. Indeed, the
very thought of Calvo's coming to Florence
to be with him sent a shudder through
Tito's frame, and he felt that the old man
would be a weight and clog. All the
chances were that he was dead, but should
events recover him to life Tito would need
his money to support his benefactor. Fate
therefore seemed to have decided that it
was best for Baldassarre to end his career
by shipwreck and death. What fate had
decided fate would achieve. Therefore

Tito bowed his will to the inevitable. He invested the five hundred florins obtained by selling his father's gems with Cennini. He determined to do nothing, and speak of his father as lost. In that sad hour Tito sold himself to the prince of evil.

If the next two months sufficed to lend a golden hue to the harvest fields and a purple cast to the vineyards, these summer months showed no other change upon Tito than that "added radiance of good fortune which is like the just perceptible perfecting of a flower after it has drunk the morning sunbeams." The youth who had landed with weather-stained tunic and hose found himself a growing influence among the leaders of Florence. Passing through the streets, his highest hopes were stirred by the cordial salutations of merchants and politicians and the grave recognition of senators and bishops. But the springs of his hope grew deeper still. Among the old patrician families, who suffered grievously from recent wars and had exchanged wealth and dignity for what seemed poverty to them, was Bardo de Bardi, who had commenced his career as a merchant, but in early life had become fascinated by the new Greek learning, and so had spent his years in the collection of rare manuscripts and precious marbles, gathering literary treasures so rich as to encourage the hope that he had made "a lasting impression upon the fast-whirling earth." From the hour when Tito, with his knowledge of the classics, entered his library, the blind scholar felt that at last he had found a secretary who could help him perfect a catalogue for these books that were to form his final monument. But to Tito the rolls and manuscripts, precious as they were, seemed as nothing in comparison with that Romola who was indeed the most beautiful girl in Florence, and had been to the blind scholar "a light in time of darkness." In those happy days oft the young Greek lingered in the library until darkness lay upon all the books, and his handsome face, his radiant spirits, his gentle, beseeching admiration, soon won the heart of this proud, shy girl. In the hour of approaching marriage Tito could scarcely believe his own good fortune. Events had fulfilled his highest hopes.

And when marriage had lent him patrician

position, by chance Tito discovered a political conspiracy. Soon an opportunity to ful-
fill a secret commission for the conspirators
filled his purse with gold. Later his guilty
knowledge made it necessary for the political leaders to widen their circle and find a
place for Tito. Soon he was a familiar figure
in all the palaces. Daily death vacates one
great man's chair. Tito waited his chance,
and then, with a single bound, leaped into
fame and fortune. Because he was not
embarrassed by conscience, he soon became
invaluable to the conspirators against the
state.

But just in the brightest hour of his new
career the shadow of Nemesis fell dark
across his path. One morning, while crossing the square, Tito met a monk, newly
arrived from Sicily. Having inquired his
name, the stranger gave Tito a packet upon
which was written, "For Tito Melema, age
twenty-three, with a dark, beautiful face,
long, dark curls, the brightest smile, and
a large onyx ring on his right forefinger."
Opening the parchment, Tito read these
words: "I am sold for a slave. They are
going to take me to Antioch. The gems

alone will ransom me." In that moment
of judgment Tito's terror was increased by
the discovery that this monk was Fra Luca,
brother to his Romola. Shivering for fear,
he cast about for help. The moment was
big with peril. There was indeed the barest
chance that Fra Luca did not know the con-
tents of the message; also the sickness that
was upon the monk might prove fatal. On
the other hand, even though his father was
alive, it was too late to sail for Antioch.
Baldassarre had had his draught of life. Tito
felt that his turn had come. Now that the
cup of joy was at his lips it was unfair to
put it away and go through life ever thirsting. Of course the five hundred florins
belonged to Baldassarre, nor did he wish
them for himself, but only for Romola.
When darkness fell, his terror increased, and
fulfilled Æschylus' words, "It is good that
fear should sit as a guardian of the soul,
forcing it into wisdom."

Since sleep was impossible, and he could
not know the result of Romola's interview with her brother until morning, and
having an unconquerable aversion to unpleasant thoughts, Tito sprang up, and,

walking through the streets, left the city behind him. He was in one of those lawless moments when the soul has no guide but desire. Also the face of a little peasant girl whom he had met in the market-place rose before him. He determined to use the evening when his fate hung in the balance by amusing himself with his new acquaintance. That night for little Tessa the flowers of the soul withered upon their branches. All the barriers that protect virtue fell in ruins.

Returning home, Tito reflected that in any event Romola would probably soon break with him. But perfect scheming demands omniscience. When the new day dawned he found that Fra Luca was dead, and had carried the guilty secret with him to the grave. Not dreaming of Tito's unfaithfulness, Romola met him with sweet abandon of love. Sorrow had clothed her with divine dignity, sweetness, and beauty. Suddenly Tito's spirit rebounded from the dread unto joy as a lithe, soft-furred young tiger leaps in its play. At once he put far away all fear. But as the days swept on this youth, who at the beginning was merely weak, moved swiftly toward shame and infamy.

Had some keen observer been blessed with the power to pierce through his outer disguise, he would have seen that this soft and beautiful body was a velvet sheath that concealed the black heart of a scoundrel. Daily this youth picked some of the ripe fruit of ease and prosperity. Nevertheless, God is just. Sins are seeds that carry in themselves harvests of coming punishment.

But the wise man saith, "Sins are like lions' cubs, and lions' whelps do grow and increase." So it happened that when months had passed Tito found his sin was a wild beast crouching at his door. One day, making his way into the center of an excited crowd, he found himself face to face with his adopted father. Fascinated and full of terror, the two men glared into each other's eyes, silent as death. Baldassarre's face was full of fury; Tito's white lips were bloodless and trembling. When an officer laid his hand upon the old man and exclaimed, "Who is this?" Tito's passion leaped forth under the inspiration of crime, and he answered, "Some madman, surely!" Transfixed by that word, Baldassarre started with pain. A magical passion seemed to leap from his eyes and to dart into the veins of Tito. But when the old man had gone, the youth quickly recovered himself, for he had "lips that could lie with dimpled smiles, eyes whose brightness infamy could not dim, cheeks that could rise from murder and not look haggard." When his companions railed him for looking as if he had seen a ghost, he excused himself and plunged into a secluded street. He felt as if "a serpent had begun to coil about his limbs." Baldassarre, living and in Florence, seemed to him the incarnation of vengeance. With bitterness he recalled that if he had but thrown himself into his father's arms one well-turned falsehood might have brought him through the crisis. But that word, "He is a madman," had revealed everything to Baldassarre. One resource was indeed possible—to turn back, to confess all to his father, to Romola, to all the world. Yet sin had so deadened his conscience that he never even thought of that.

Not until weeks had passed did he understand why Baldassarre had delayed his vengeance. The old man was waiting for an hour of publicity, when this traitor, this hated favorite of blind fortune, was surrounded by chief men, on whose favor he depended. One evening Tito was the guest of honor at Rucellai's palace. At the moment when the festivities were at their height Baldassarre suddenly entered the room. When Tito turned pale and trembled, the silence of death fell upon all. Baldassarre said: "There is a man here who is a scoundrel, a liar, a robber. I took him from beggary when he was a child. I was a father to him. I made him a scholar. My head has lain hard that he might have a pillow. Shipwrecked, he left me in slavery. He sold my gems, and when I came he denied me." Amazed, doubting, bewildered, the guests looked from Baldassarre to Tito, not knowing this end. But the excitement was too much for the old man. Broken-hearted, now the strings of his mind also snapped. A moment later all memory passed from him. Servants led him away. Then the banqueters expressed sympathy with Tito that this crazy old man had fastened his hatred upon one so innocent. But if the banquet went on, Tito's heart was palpitating. The wine tasted no better "than if it had been blood." For safety he had paid a heavy price. That night Tito trembled, and felt that the stars blazed anger at him. The earth had become dust, and the heavens were iron and brass. He was now an exile from Eden. Angels with swords of flame kept the gates of Paradise against him.

Yet night and sleep recovered Tito's old-time caution and coolness. If all else failed, flight at least was left. Of late, indeed, events had not gone well with Tito. Always of extravagant tastes, his expenses were heavy, and the peasant girl and her two babes had cost him much money. Flight to Venice or Paris meant increased expenditure. Then it was that the man bethought himself of Romola's father's library. At first the very thought of treachery to the dead filled him with sickening terror. For half a century the scholar had used the fruit of his toil to collect these manuscripts and parchments. Only a few weeks before the cardinal had promised a building in which the collection might be preserved, thus handing forward the name of Bardo de Bardi. Grievous necessity was upon Tito. Finding he had a legal right to sell the books, he at once arranged with the agent of the Duke of Milan to visit the library in Romola's absence.

That night he asked the young wife what possible good those rolls and books could do if kept in one building under her father's name more than if divided. Scattered through various cities would they not bring light and inspiration to many people? When the Grecian scholars with their manuscripts fled before the Turks, was not the loss of Constantinople the gain of the whole world? An hour later Romola knew that the library had already been sold to the Duke of Milan, and that Tito had broken the solemn pledge made to her dying father. In that moment the rich, warm blood in her veins turned to molten steel. Her love, too, died forever. Affection was succeeded by hatred and contempt. When the morning dawned over the city the young wife knew that her life, that had seemed a beauteous temple for happiness and peace, had become a ruined heap. He who had entered her life as an angel of light now stood forth a demon, clothed with shame and infamy.

And now this man who had become a traitor to his home becomes a traitor to his country. The youth who at the outset would have stepped aside from the path lest he hurt a young bird was now capable of treading the breath from a smiling child for the sake of his own safety. His was the "sharp mind in a velvet sheath," and his also the iron heart to wield the keen blade. Since Romola chose to assume an air of lofty superiority, with sneers, he decided to abandon her and flee to some unknown city where he might forget the past and begin life afresh. If flight demanded a long purse, opportunity offered a way for filling his purse with gold. His long and close acquaintance with Romola's uncle made him the possessor of Nello's hope of seeing the liberty of Florence restored. Going before the prince he sold the information that brought several patriots to their death and lined his belt with gold and gems. But if his falsehood prospered, his fear waxed also, for fear had become a habit with him. Not that he feared Baldassarre, for confessedly the old man was crazy. Not that he feared Romola's suspicion, for she knew all his treachery. The scaffold, too, had silenced Nello's lips forever. From habit Tito now was the slave of terror.

One night, returning home, he found rioting going on in the street, and heard the roar of the mob that was preparing to attack San Marco. At once he made his preparations for flight. When the morning came, Tito descended the steps looking nearly as brilliant as the day he had crossed that threshold to meet Romola. The thought of his old life was now cast off, and that he was about to enter a new one lent him strange excitement. He was to meet his man and the mules beyond the Ponte Vecchio. Hurrying to the bridge, he saw the streets thereabout filled with rioters. It was vexatious, but he must make his way through the mob. Once on the bridge, he found himself surrounded by a group of men whom he recognized as friends of the senators he had betrayed. In a sudden flash he knew that these angry men were about to avenge their friends, slain through his treachery. At sight of Tito their angry yells and execrations increased. Plainly death was just at hand. In a moment his hat was off, his mantle torn in shreds. Suddenly **Tito** drew forth his purse, and scattering the gold and gems, took advantage of the open space and leaped from the bridge into the Arno below. Once before his fine swimming had saved his life. Diving under the water, the youth hoped that the crowd would think him drowned. If he could but swim beyond the bridges, there was still a chance of life. On and on he swam, passing one bridge after another, until he was on the outskirts of the city. But excitement had spent his strength, and he had been up all the night before. The current now began to have its way with him. Scarcely conscious, his feet felt the shore. But unwittingly the swimmer was not alone. One onlooker had seen Tito spring into the river—Baldassarre, his avenger. The old man was on the bank, keeping pace with the swimmer, and when at last Tito approached the reeds and fell, half fainting, among the rushes, Baldassarre leaped like a tiger upon the unconscious youth.

When the swimmer's eyes opened and the light of consciousness vibrated in them, he looked into the eyes of Baldassarre, but he knew not whether it was life or death that brought him into the presence of his father. In that moment of recognition the remnant of strength in the old man leaped into flame. Kneeling upon the youth, he clutched his throat tighter and tighter. Long after the eyes had become rigid and the flesh cold the avenger was still there, not daring to trust this seeming death. Many hours later a peasant saw a startling object lying upon the river's bank. The aged man had fallen forward, his dead clutch still upon the other's throat. It was not possible to sep- arate them, so the two bodies, now united by hate and vengeance as once by love, were carried back to the great piazza for identification. "It is the prisoner who clutched Tito and convulsed him with ter- ror," said Piero. "It is the old man who appeared at my banquet," said Rucellai. Not so. Those fingers upon the throat of Tito were the fingers of Eternal Justice. For justice is like "the kingdom of God—it is not without us as a fact; it is within us as a great yearning."

Since Tito's time, centuries have come

and gone. The house of the De Bardi is no longer known in Florence. The old booths are now in ruins. But could these tombs that hold the sacred dust of the blind scholar and his beautiful daughter give up their dead; could the martyred lips of Savonarola again break forth in speech, these would have one message and one warning: we knew a youth once who was bright, and beautiful, and full of promise. So kind was he and gentle that at first the mere thought of cruelty made him ill. But because he tried to slip out of everything unpleasant, and always chose the selfish path, he came to do deeds black and infamous. For the mere hope of becoming rich and prosperous, he was faithless to every trust. Yet what he sowed he reaped. He sowed treachery toward his city, and reaped the anger of the mob. He sowed selfishness toward his home, and reaped the contempt of a noble wife. He sowed ingratitude toward his father, and reaped a hatred that choked out his life.

Therefore, beware of the beginnings of evil. Once disease hath wiped the bloom of health and beauty from the cheeks of youth, the blush can never be restored.

Tamper not with conscience; it is the soul's compass. Reflect that the little sins that seem to-day like the soft balls of fur, named lions' cubs, fit for playthings, will to-morrow be wild beasts crouching at thy door. And if passion leaping from its lair hath overcome thee, make instant confession, that the soul may recover its purity. For man may be born again. Christ's love and life and death can consume the soul's transgression. God's mercy can forgive. His deep seas can bury forever sins forever forsaken. But if trifling sins oft repeated have seared thy conscience, then beware! Beware! Beware! A thousand times beware! if sin no longer cuts a deep, bloody gash in thy heart! Whatsoever a man soweth that shall he also reap. "For God will bring every word into judgment, with every secret thing, whether it be good or whether it be evil."

IV

Hawthorne's "Scarlet Letter" and the
Retributive Workings of Conscience—
A Study of the Necessity and Nobility
of Repentance, and the Confession of
Sin

There can be, if I forebode aright, no power, short of the Divine mercy, to disclose, whether by uttered words or by type or emblem, the secrets that may be buried with a human heart. The heart, making itself guilty of such secrets, must perforce hold them, until the day when all hidden things shall be revealed. Nor have I so read or interpreted Holy Writ as to understand the disclosure of human thoughts and deeds, then to be made, is intended as a part of the retribution. That, surely, were a shallow view of it. No; these revelations, unless I greatly err, are meant merely to promote the intellectual satisfaction of all intelligent beings, who will stand waiting, on that day, to see the dark problem of this life made plain. A knowledge of men's hearts will be needful to the completest solution of that problem. And I conceive, moreover, that the hearts holding such miserable secrets as you speak of will yield them up, at that last day, not with reluctance, but with a joy unutterable.—*Scarlet Letter, p. 161.*

IV

HAWTHORNE'S "SCARLET LETTER" AND THE RETRIBUTIVE WORKINGS OF CONSCIENCE—A STUDY OF THE NECESSITY AND NOBILITY OF REPENTANCE, AND THE CONFESSION OF SIN

Conceding preëminency in morals and reason to the Hebrew and Greek peoples, giving the first place in law and philosophy to the Latin and German races, let us also confess that England holds a unique position in the realm of literature. In the history of letters the names most illustrious, perhaps, are names of English origin. If the critics mention three poets of the first order—Homer, Dante, and Shakespeare— the greatest of these is the bard of Avon. If scholars make a second group for Æschylus, Virgil, Milton, and Goethe, the English poet easily heads this list. If German thinkers are preëminent in the realm of modern philosophy, it was Francis Bacon who developed the principles of the inductive system. In the material world, nations from time to time exhibit their tools, art, and industries. Should an era ever come when the great races hold an exposition of genius, and display the achievements of their poets, essayists, and scientists, the English exhibit will ask for a large and generous section, while America's contribution will need but a modest corner. In this court of honor, Emerson the essayist, Lowell the scholar, and Longfellow the poet, Motley the historian, and Hawthorne the novelist, will doubtless obtain recognition and high praise. Confessedly, from the view-point of fiction, the author of "The Scarlet Letter" is the first of American authors, and takes high rank among the ten great novelists. Renowned as a literary artist, he is also unique as a teacher of morals. His one theme, never forgotten and always insisted upon, is conscience and the retributive workings of justice.

In the "House of Seven Gables," Hawthorne exhibits one generation as sowing sins that are seeds whose harvests of penalty are garnered by generations that follow after. In the "Marble Faun," he portrays Donatello as "less man than child, less child than animal," who seems a youth buoyant and mirthful, as unconscious as a big-eyed fawn in the forest, whose conscience, through sin and crime, at last rouses the youth into self-recognition and full manhood. In his "Septimius Felton," Hawthorne suggests that sins may have consequences that reach forward unto immortality. When a scientist has slain his friend, influenced in part by remorse, he returns to the spot, to find upon the grave a plant with blossoms, crimson and gorgeous beyond words, having leaves heavy with potent juices, from which he distilled an elixir of immortal life, only to find himself immortal in woe, agony, and remorse. For, like all minds of the first order of genius, Hawthorne concerns himself with the great problems of the soul. If Æschylus exhibits the sinning of Agamemnon as pursued by furies, and Virgil made his hero to be pursued by fate, Hawthorne makes conscience to pursue Dimmesdale.

Our generation has journeyed far from the

Puritan era, with its grim justice and its relentless penalties, but Hawthorne dwelt beneath the dark shadow of the Iron Age. His intellect and imagination were alike fascinated by the Puritan idea of justice. Grim men and stern those Puritans named Cotton Mather and Jonathan Edwards, having neither part nor lot in human infirmities, and insensible alike to pleasure and pain. Generations of these worthies, with their iron rigor, entered into, and, as M. Montégut says, "slowly filtered" through Hawthorne, and the precious drops fell into that vessel named "The Scarlet Letter." By way of contrast, this study of conscience differs from the sentimental novels of to-day as an oak tree differs from the hyacinth, as a battle-ship differs from a circus wrestler. Our age, with its flabby conscience and its languid morals, does well to ponder Hawthorne's pages, to the end that its youth may have "more iron in the blood, more brawn and sinew in the intellect, more justice in our ethics and politics, more judgment in the theology."* The revival of art and letters seems to have fully come.

* "The Eternal Atonement."—Hitchcock.

Society now needs to add a revival of law, justice, and the moral imperative.

If Kant emphasized the starry heavens and the moral law; if Daniel Webster emphasized the thought of personal responsibility to God, Hawthorne believed the greatest thought that can occupy the human mind is the thought of justice and its retributive workings through conscience. Doubtless there are a thousand problems that compete for the attention of youth; but for men grown mature and strong, life offers no more momentous question than this: Can the soul, injured by temptation and scarred by sin, ever recover its pristine strength and beauty? Is it true that the breach that guilt has made in the soul may never be repaired, but only guarded and watched, while always by the broken wall there lurks "the stealthy tread of a foe who waits to renew his unforgotten triumphs"? Is there no place of recovery, though man seek it long with tears? "I do not know," answers the old Greek. "I do not know that God has any right to forgive sins." But Dante, having affirmed that man cannot forgive himself, thinks that sin may be consumed, and therefore makes the transgressor walk up a stairway of red-hot marble that pain may consume his iniquities. Though Hawthorne dwelt in a grim, dark era, for him there was sunlight on the top of the mountains. The summer shower, falling softly upon the banks of violets, cleanses the soot from the blossoms. In the deep forest glen a pure spring gushes, and into the deep pool wild birds plunge to brighten their dull plumage. And Hawthorne felt that somewhere life holds a fountain divine for cleansing the dust from the soul's wings. Baring to us all the secrets of the human heart, and portraying the gradual unfolding of pain and penalty, at last he affirms that the sinning soul may recover its native simplicity and dignity through repentance and confession. Therefore, at the very gates of the jail into which the prisoner enters, Hawthorne made a rosebush grow, with thorns indeed to typify the sharp pains that society inflicts upon the wrongdoer, but with blossoms, too, offering fragrance to the prisoner as he goes in, and suggesting that if the petals fall through the frosts of to-day, these falling petals, passing into the root, will reappear in the richer blossoms of to-morrow. As if another life might recover the disasters of this; as if, no matter what man's harshness, great nature and nature's God hold a wide, deep pity that can atone, forgive, and save.

Recognizing that the pivotal point in David's career is the moment of his confession in the temple; that through public repentance Saul, the murderer, became Paul, the apostle; that Judas, upon returning to the high priest and flinging down the thirty pieces of silver, almost wins a place in our regard; Hawthorne believed that everything in his drama of the soul must be made to turn upon the open confession of sin. Therefore, among many possible transgressions he selects the one sin that has the most reasons against acknowledgment, and the one man in the community who would suffer the most by telling the truth. And that his lesson might be the more convincing he lends a thousand extenuations to the wrongdoers.

Hawthorne exhibits this daughter of beauty and sorrow as the target and wreck of misfortune. He takes us back to an old English town, to a decayed house of

stone, with a broken shield of arms above
its door in token of its gentility.   He shows
us an anxious but revered father, whose
spirit has been broken by misfortune; a
beauteous mother, overzealous for those she
loves; a daughter, as yet a mere child in
years and heart, who has suddenly developed into the fullness of a glorious womanhood, having all those gifts of rich, warm
beauty and tall, full figure that lend the
note of distinction to the daughter of a
patrician race.

Then, at a critical moment, we see a man
of wealth entering the scene and offering
to repair the family's misfortunes; a man
well stricken in years; a mere animated
bookworm, who takes advantage of the
daughter's inexperience and the parents'
misfortunes to urge the opportunity of
home and wealth. Mocking the young
girl's protestations that her heart held no
love for him, by sheer force of will and
wealth the old scholar carried her off to a
continental city, with its strange language,
its tall, gray, forbidding houses, its dark
cathedral, and in that lonely land the frightened girl came to seem like a prisoner,

whose jailer was the old scholar carrying the
key to the cell that shut her in.   One day,
when the few English families in Amster-
dam were about to sail for the New World,
this bookworm, unwilling to tear himself from
its libraries, placed the young wife on board
the ship and sent her away, friendless and
uncared for, save as gold lends protection,
while he stayed behind to feed his hungry
dream of knowledge.   On the wharf he
promised to follow on a later ship.   When
months had passed and the ship in which
he had sailed was not heard from, this girl,
whose life had fed upon the scholar's time-
worn materials "like a tuft of green moss
on a crumbling wall," under new expe-
riences opened into the fullness of a rich
womanhood and found a happiness before
undreamed of.   When the ship landed in
Boston, she entered upon two new worlds.

If once a deformed and selfish scholar
had guided her studies, she now passed
under the influence of a noble youth, trained
in England's greatest university, with rare
native gifts and scholarly acquirements that
lent their possessor unique eminence.   How
deeply did she regret that irretrievable mis-

take. How fierce her hatred of that old man who had first deluded and then deserted her! What bitterness toward the parents who had done her so grievous a wrong! A thousand times, also, young Dimmesdale, the scholar, indicted that grim Puritanism that made marriage impossible for this deserted daughter of grace and beauty. A thousand times, too, he indicted Providence for cruelty in stretching forth to him the cup of joy only to withdraw it. Society's laws shut him in like a grim and beetling fortress, against whose granite walls he vainly struck his bleeding forehead. But if pain and disappointment weakened the youth, suffering lent the woman strength. In that Iron Age for a man to transgress the marriage law meant not simply disgrace, but the dungeon, and death by hanging. So the woman swore her fellow-sufferer's lips to silence. Alone she walked her "Via Dolorosa." Alone she went forth into the darkness and the pitiless storm that now burst upon her devoted head. Bearing her own pain unaided, she tried to bear another's anguish also. Solitary in the majesty of her sacrifice and the beauty of her love, she seems indeed like our "Lady of Sorrows."

If motives of fear, pride, and love itself united to hold the wrongdoer back from open acknowledgment, Providence ordained that events should compel a full confession. According to the grim Puritan code the offender against the home received the brand of a red-hot iron upon the forehead. But when the governor and those who had charge of the moral interests of the community counseled together, the young pastor made so earnest a plea for mercy rather than justice that the rulers, in a lenient moment, substituted a scarlet letter upon the dress for the red brand upon the forehead. They also sent forth a solemn proclamation commanding the people to assemble in the market-place, that the most holy community of Massachusetts might "show itself righteous by dragging iniquity into the sunshine." Then straightway the husbandman forgot his tools and the artisan his task. Gathering about the pillory, the people found there assembled the governor, the counselors, the two pastors, and the magistrate. When silence had fallen upon the multitude, an aged teacher arose, who, in the face of high heaven, and in the presence of all the people, charged home the blackness of the transgression and the necessity of making known the name of him who had led another into a sin so grievous.

It seemed also the refinement of cruelty that the duty of urging her to full speech and open confession fell upon him whom she had pledged to silence, lest his confession bring infamy upon his sacred profession and incur the certain death that she had escaped by reason of her innocent child. Dramatic indeed that scene when the sufferer from his desk urged his fellow-sufferer on her scaffold to believe that it was mistaken pity and kindness not to compel the wrongdoer to leave his high position and mount the pedestal of ignominy, rather than go through life hiding a guilty secret; that every consideration of mercy bade her give the bitter and wholesome cup to him who lacked strength to take it for himself— an appeal so broken and so heartrending as to cause all hearers to wait with breathless expectancy for the wrongdoer to rise up and publish his error. But when neither the plea of the friend, the threat of an enemy, nor the command of the magistrate availed for wringing from the sufferer's lips any word, save the broken exclamation that she would never speak, but would fain bear another's agony as well as her own, then from the lips of Dimmesdale came the startled exclamation, "Oh, wondrous strength and generosity of a woman's heart! She will not speak!"

In that moment the man's dumb lips were nigh to full speech. If the all-sacrificing love that would die in another's stead melted even the grim magistrates, that all-enduring love broke the heart of Dimmesdale. Every instinct of manhood and honor bade him lift the shield above this shrinking sufferer, upon whose head the very skies seemed to rain crushing pains and burning penalties. But the shadow of the scaffold struck terror through him, and back he shrank into silence. If the angels of his better nature bade him accept the bitter cup of death, the demons pushed back the cup of pain saying: "You may escape the prison cell and avoid the scaffold. All yet may be well." That night this daughter of suffering, sleeping in a dungeon, seemed the child of liberty, while Dimmesdale, who seemed a free man, became the bond slave of sin and the prisoner of fear and remorse. Listening, he might have heard the laughter of demons rejoicing over the wreck and ruin of a man's soul. From that hour he was a target for the slings and arrows of an outraged conscience.

To the proverb, "Justice holds an even scale," must be added the words, "Justice never slumbers." Transgressions are self-punishing. Once men taught that God from time to time descends upon evil-doers to execute divine wrath and penalty. Now we know that every sin journeys forward fully equipped with instruments for its own punishment. Our earth is too small to make wrongdoing safe. Be the speck upon an apple ever so minute, the decay upon one side will journey round and meet the corruption upon the other side. Oft eternal justice seems to shrink our earth to the size of an apple, until at last every wrongdoer and his victim stand face to face.

So it came about that one day the old scholar appeared in the market-place at the time of Hester's ignominious exposure. When he beheld the woman in whom he had hoped to find embodied the warmth and cheerfulness of home set up as a type of sin before the people, "a creeping horror twisted itself across his features, like a snake riding over them." Seeking to avoid the contagion of her dishonor, he resolved not to be pilloried on her pedestal of shame. From that hour the old man determined to give himself to the discovery of Hester's unknown lover. "I shall know him," he whispered. "In his presence some hidden voice will whisper his secret." Having sworn secrecy upon the part of the one person who knew him, he withdrew his name from the roll of mankind, and "vanished out of life as completely as if he indeed lay at the bottom of the ocean, to which rumor had consigned him."

Taking the name of Roger Chillingworth, he used his knowledge of medicine to strengthen his disguise. As skilled physicians were rare in the New World, he was soon counted as a brilliant acquisition to the colony. One day, when the governor returned from a visit to his pastor, he sent for the old physician, and besought him to use his skill in the interests of one who seemed about to fall in death. If many accounted for the paleness of the young man's cheek by his overstudy, by his frequent fasts and vigilance, others feared that the disease was deeperseated, for "his form grew emaciated, his voice held a certain melancholy prophecy of decay, and in every moment of sudden alarm he was seen to put his hand over his heart, with first a flush and then a paleness indicative of pain."

Once he had taken up his sojourn beneath Dimmesdale's roof, the old physician became strangely suspicious. Hours there were when this youth's spirit seemed clothed with such freshness, fragrance, and dewy purity of thought that his speech seemed the speech of an angel. If at such times Chillingworth turned his suspicions toward the magistrate or merchant, he always returned to Dimmesdale. Prying into the young man's heart, he burrowed there like a miner searching for hidden treasure. Leading the scholar to talk of his early life, his studies, ambitions, and discouragements, the old man watched for some hint that might confirm his secret thought. Yet at such times he followed the speaker with as cautious a tread and as wary an outlook as a thief entering a chamber where a man lies half asleep. One day, when several years had passed, the old physician brought in some poisonous herbs and roots. Asked whence they came, the physician answered that they grew out of the grave in which was buried a man who held a guilty secret.

When Dimmesdale replied that perchance the sufferer earnestly desired to speak, but could not, and affirmed his belief "that in the last great judgment day every heart that holds a miserable secret will yield it up, not with reluctance, but with a joy unutterable," Hawthorne says a strange light gleamed out of the old man's eyes, like one of those flashes of ghastly hue that darted from Bunyan's awful doorway in the hillside and quivered on the pilgrim's face. Afterward it came about that the physician gave his patient a quieting draught, for sleep with Dimmesdale had long been as fitful as a bird that hops from bough to bough. When he had fallen into a deep, deathlike torpor the old physician drew back the vestment from the sleeper's bosom, and turned away with a wild look of wonder, joy, and horror. "Had a man seen old Roger Chillingworth at that moment of ecstasy," says Hawthorne, "he would have had no need to ask how Satan deports himself when a precious soul is lost to heaven and won into his community."

Now that he knew the guilty man's secret, the malicious enemy, under pretense of friendship, proceeded to wreak upon his sufferer such vengeance as had never before been conceived by an enemy. He became the chief inquisitor in that torture chamber named the sufferer's heart. Every morning for a few minutes he stretched his victim upon the rack. Every evening he lifted his hand, and by suggestions caused a thousand ghastly phantoms of death, or, still more awful, shame, to rise up and point their fingers at his breast. But conscience was the chiefest scourge. For Dimmesdale's was not the cold, hard, iron intellect that, when long time hath passed, can leave both the sin and the memory thereof in the forgotten past. To his keen intellect he added sensitive spiritual nature, moral sympathy, unwonted powers of affection and aspiration—the temperament of which martyrs have always been made.

Oft, looking out upon his audience, he told his hearers that he was blacker than the blackest, his whole life a lie and a delusion, his heart full of sins that were red like scarlet. And yet his fame for righteousness grew more and more. In a secret chest, under lock and key, he hid a bloody scourge, with which he plied his shoulders. Fasting by day, he kept long vigils by night, until his brain reeled and his strength failed. In one of those half-unconscious hours he saw a herd of demons drawing near, beckoning him to join their company. Once, when an angel band approached, as if for convoy, the celestial beings started back in horror and fled, for they recognized his guilty secret. Saddest of all, the ghost of his revered mother approached, only to pass by without casting a single pitying look behind.

One midnight hour, while he kept his vigil, a sudden flash of lightning revealed the scaffold, and something suggested that upon that spot perchance he might find rest

and peace. Softly creeping down the stairway, he lifted the latch, stole out into the
night, made his way to the pillory, and
ascended the scaffold, now blackened by the
storms of seven long years. For his soul
was thirsting for confession as pilgrims in a
desert thirst for the spring of living water.
When sin warps the soul out of line, repentance springs it back again to its normal
place. He who has pondered long life's
deepest problems knows that memory holds
no dearer recollection than hours when the
erring child moves from sin toward confession and forgiveness. Disobedient, the
child fears the parent's disapproval. Dread-
ing the discovery, it conceals the sin through
deceit. Soon the sweetness of the stolen
pleasure passes away. Remorse makes a
dark cloud to overshadow the child. Each
moment increases the gloom. And when
the darkness falls and the prayers are said,
and the light is turned out, and the mother's kiss leaves the child alone, with solitude
comes increased sorrow. Because its first
lie is a sin greater than it can bear, the child
calls aloud, and flinging itself into the arms
of the returning mother, in a wild, passion-

ate abandon of tears and sobs pours forth the full story of its sin, and, mingling its torrent with the parent's tears, is cleansed in that deep fountain named the mother's heart. What hour in life holds a happiness so deep and sweet as that hour of confession and forgiveness for the child, when it falls asleep, having recovered its simplicity? And men are but children grown tall and strong. If the years increase, the sins of maturity also gather volume and terror. Dimmesdale's soul was thirsting for confession. Full speech would have recovered him to his native beauty and simplicity. But silence was fast bringing him to the verge of lunacy.

Not until seven full years had passed by did Hester suddenly realize that the old physician had discovered Dimmesdale's secret, and, fiendlike, had tortured his victim to the verge of lunacy. If once she had been unequal to a combat with the keen scholar, suffering and struggle had now lent her strength, while the old man's hatred and revenge had made him weak. Seeking an interview, she told Chillingworth plainly that she had determined to reveal his name, even if it cost the life of his victim. Then she stretched out hands of help and succor toward one from whom she had been separated for these many years. But death itself would have been less painful than that meeting. Grievous indeed the shock of the discovery that his enemy had violated all the sanctities of his soul! Little wonder that for an hour the very foundations of reason trembled for the broken-hearted man.

Shattered in health, temptations sprang up and threatened to destroy what manhood was left. Then the woman's strength lent guidance and counsel. Surely the boundless forest could hide him from the gaze of Roger Chillingworth. The sea would bear him to the Old World, where perchance he might rebuild his ruined life. On the morrow, indeed, a ship was to sail for England. Once the decision was made to sail with it, Dimmesdale felt his old life fall like a worm-eaten garment from his shoulders. Rising up from that interview, he who had been sick, sin-stained, sorrow-blackened, felt almost joy again. His was the exultation of the prisoner who had just escaped from the dungeon of his own heart. When

the night fell it found him fully prepared
for flight upon the morrow. Yet that hour
was big with peril. Never had there been
a darker moment in this man's career. For
years the angels of his better nature had
been seeking to draw him to that one place
where he might recover manhood—the scaffold. And now he was about to put the
ocean between himself and that pillory
where he ought to stand. That night, while
all men slept, God heaved this man's soul
"like an ocean." It was as if the angels
divine had redoubled their efforts, making
one last, long struggle to redeem this sufferer back to truth and his native purity and
beauty.

When the momentous day dawned for
Dimmesdale it brought the duties of the
election ceremony. In the morning a
solemn procession of the citizens was
formed. To the sound of military music
soldiers clad in burnished steel marched
toward the church, where solemn ceremonies
lent dignity to the ballot and clothed the
citizen with the rank of sovereign. When
the governor and his counselors were seated
within the sacred building, and silence had

fallen upon the multitude without, through the open windows of the church came the voice of the speaker. Under the stimulus of his excitement the powerful intellect of Dimmesdale now took up his enfeebled body and lent it strength. And yet his physician knew that already he was stricken with death and was tottering to his end. Standing beside the pillory that seven years before had witnessed her ignominy, Hester, listening, heard his voice, with its old, rich, deep tones, indeed rising higher and higher, yet underneath the full tones she heard the low, pathetic undertones of pain. In prophetic mood the speaker was forecasting the future of the colony, and he prophesied a high and glorious destiny for the young republic. Borne forward upon his tumultuous speech, the hearers felt that such inspiration had never before been lent to mortal lips. It was as if "an angel in his journey through the skies had stayed his flight, hanging above the people, at once a shadow and a splendor, and had cast down a shower of golden truths upon the beholders." For Dimmesdale it was the proudest eminence to which gifts of intellect, vast learning, and great eloquence could exalt a public teacher. And when the speaker had completed, the enthusiasm was beyond all bounds.

The solemn ceremony of the day completed, the orator took the governor's arm, heading the procession as it marched out. But once he was in the open air, Dimmesdale turned to the pillory and swiftly ascended the scaffold. Then a great awe fell upon the multitude. In his excitement the old physician sprang forward, whispering: "Madman! what doest thou? All shall be well. I can yet save you. Do not bring infamy upon your sacred profession." Dimmesdale, now triumphant over sin, replied, "Tempter, thou art too late; with God's help I will escape thee." To which his enemy answered, "In all the world there was no one place so secret—no high place nor lowly place where thou couldst have escaped me — save this scaffold." Then, supported by one beside whom he should have stood seven years before, in the presence of all the people, he tore off his cloak of lies blackening his name—not knowing that he cleansed it—dishonoring his reputation as a moral teacher — not knowing that Christianity at last had become powerful upon his lips. In that moment of bitter repentance, like David, the sin-dying man recovered his soul to its native simplicity and beauty. Stricken with awe, the behold-ers saw, as it were, a great light. Then the flame of life for this dying man burned low in the socket, quivered one moment—then went out forever. When a great ship goes down at sea, the swirling currents eddy round with low, deep murmurs, and when the multitude at last broke into the voice of wonder, deep answered unto deep, while their murmurs rolled after the departed spirit.

The centuries have come and gone, the scaffold now is dust, the scarlet letter is a legend; yet through the silent air there falls the still, small voice, whispering: "Behold, thou art the man." If God's good provi-dence hath held thee back from such suffer-ing and sin as overtook thy fellow-mortal, surely some selfish thought, some unholy purpose, hath lent its stain to thy secret life. Alas! alas! for him whose prayer is the Pharisee's of old, "God, I thank thee that I am not as other men are, extortioners, unjust, adulterers!" Happy, thrice happy, those who smite upon the breast, saying, "God be merciful to me, a sinner!" Thou child of strength and youth, hast thou defrauded thine employers? Think not by flight to escape the demons who pursue thee. Flee not *from*, but *to* thine employer! Making full restitution, lose thou his regard, and recover thine own respect and God's approval. Thou prodigal son, far hast thou wandered from thy mother's knee! Long hast thou dwelt in Circe's palace! Deeply hast thou drank of cups of flame! Know that the path of repentance alone will lead thee back to thy Father's house! There is welcome, mercy, healing, and recovery for thy wrecked and ruined life. Thou daughter of beauty, whose crown is loveliness, thou of the disheveled locks, with the lights and shadows still upon thy mantling hair, the time was that, walking in thy father's garden, the anemones beneath thy feet were not so sweet as thy pure heart. Wing-caught art thou, like a bird in the thicket! But know that there is one heart that aches for thee, the Divine Heart, who knows all, who understands all, who will forgive all, who will make thee to forget all! Thou who hast gone through the thunder of life's battle and who dost sit now upon thy western piazza, waiting for life's sun to set, even thy wounds may be healed, thy hurts be helped, for thou mayst return to the days when the heart is young. For men high and men low, for men on the throne, for men in the dungeon and on the gibbet, for all wounded, bleeding, broken hearts, there is welcome, healing, and recovery. One duty is thine—repentance and confession. One place in the universe there is where thou mayst escape thy sin—the place called Calvary. Climbing thy pillory, fling thine arms about the cross. To flee from Christ, flee thou to Him! "Behold thou the Lamb of God, who taketh away the sin of the world."

V

Victor Hugo's " Les Miserables "—The
Battle of the Angels and the Demons
for Man's Soul.   How Jean Valjean
was Recovered from Passion and Sin to
Christian Service and Self-sacrifice

There was a moment during which he regarded his future. Denounce himself! great heavens! give himself up! He thought with immense despair of all that he must give up, of all that he must resume. He would be forced to bid adieu to this good, pure, radiant life—to the respect of all classes—to honor, to liberty! He would no longer walk about the fields, he would not hear the birds sing in May, nor give alms to the little children! He would no longer feel the sweetness of glances of gratitude and love fixed upon him! He would leave this little house, which he had built, and his little bedroom. All appeared charming to him at this moment. He would no longer read those books or write at the little deal table; his old servant would no longer bring up his coffee in the morning. Great God! instead of all this there would be the gang, the red jacket, the chain on his foot, fatigue, the dungeon, the camp-bed, and all the horrors he knew! At his age, after all he had borne! And whatever he might do, he ever fell back into this crushing dilemma, which was the basis of his reverie —remain in paradise, and become a demon there; or re-enter hell, and become an angel? Thus the wretched soul writhed in agony! Eighteen hundred years before this unhappy man, the mysterious being in whom are embodied all the sanctities and sufferings of humanity, had also, while the olive trees shuddered in the fierce wind of the infinite, long put away with his hand the awful cup which appeared to him, dripping with shadow and overflowing with darkness in the starry depths.

I presume that all of you consider me worthy of pity? Great God! when I think of what I was on the point of doing, I consider myself worthy of envy. Still, I should have preferred that all this had not taken place.—*Fantine, pp. 350, 351, 352, 416.*

V

VICTOR HUGO'S "LES MISERABLES"—THE
BATTLE OF THE ANGELS AND THE
DEMONS FOR MAN'S SOUL. HOW JEAN
VALJEAN WAS RECOVERED FROM PAS-
SION AND SIN TO CHRISTIAN SERVICE
AND SELF-SACRIFICE

Literature includes four epic poems of the
first rank of genius. In the order of time
these are the "Iliad," the "Æneid," the
"Divine Comedy," and the "Paradise
Lost." Strangely enough, these primary
springs of education for four nations have
one and the same theme—the divineness of
man's soul, its loss, and its recovery also.
Homer's "Iliad" sings the wrath of Peleus's
son, the consequent woes that overtook the
Greeks, and shows how one sin can pull
down a structure that many virtues must
build up. Virgil's "Æneid" is an allegory
of the ages of man, telling us youth wanders
far astray, while maturity seeks out harbors

of refuge. In the "Divine Comedy" "ten silent centuries find their voice," while Dante sings of the soul's injury by sin, its purification, and also its perfection. Milton, in his sublime epic, looks out upon man's tragic career, and follows the "Lost Paradise" with the "Paradise Found," trying "to justify the ways of God to men." To these poems must be added two works that are not epic in form. The "Idylls of the King" is Tennyson's "Paradise Lost," with this all-controlling thought—if one error ruins the soul, a divine Friend there is who toils tirelessly to recover the undimmed splendor. In the realm of prose, Victor Hugo's "Les Miserables" represents the first attempt in fiction to show that if sin dims the divine image, conscience disturbs the soul with sore discontent, while Christ never despairs of making bad men good, but toils ever on until publican and outcast alike stand forth, clothed with every courage, every heroism, and every virtue, being of goodness all compact.

When our literary critics call the roll of the great novels, with striking unanimity they give "Les Miserables" the first place.

Victor Hugo's "Les Miserables"

In this book Victor Hugo portrays those representatives of society called legislators, judges, bishops, policemen, the lover and the child, as lesser planets, moving round a giant soul who is "the incarnation of all the social misery of his time." In these pages we see how God uses conscience to waken a dead soul and "plague the sinful man with dark despair" until the conscience that first made a coward of a bad man at last makes a hero of a good man. The problem which this book treats is the most perplexing problem that has ever faced thinking men. The giants of strength and intellect and the children of ease, friendship, and opportunity occasion little anxiety to philosophers. But the submerged classes, with their mendicancy, drunkenness, poverty, and crime, fill the heart of good men with anguish, and even with despair. Over against these children of good fortune, who live lives sheltered by love, are those who seem chosen to misfortune, ingratitude, and shame. These seem to go through life pelted with troubles as with fiery hail. Feeling that they are unloved by God and unregarded by men, they wander forth like King Lear with uncovered heads into life's darkness and the driving storm. For whether we are citizens of Chicago or New York, citizens of London or Paris, we must confess that it is but a step from the parliament houses and the palaces to regions where men are huddled together in tenement-houses like beasts, eating, drinking, working, cursing, dying in the same close, foul den, over whom vices and sin sweep with the force of destroying waves.

On lord mayor's day in London, the city fathers and merchants, lords and ladies, clothed in purple and fur, drove in stately procession from St. Paul's to the house of parliament. On the morning after Dives had his procession, Lazarus went forth for his parade. Men and women out of work walked in a procession of dumb despair, the men with gaunt and hungry faces, the women and children emaciated and with tattered garments, their strength anger, their bread bitterness, their nights despair. Every great city includes among its people multitudes that are debased to the level of beasts and are as ignorant as savages. Looking out upon this multitude that goes throbbing, blundering, falling, bleeding through life, the man who loves his kind oft cries out: "Does God behold this piteous tragedy? How can He stand the sight of this anguish? Has He, who once was kindly, become cold? Has He, who once was near, become vague and afar off? Having lingered long over Christ's idea of man and God, Victor Hugo determined to write the story of God's pathetic struggle to recover man from ignorance, squalor, and crime to his pristine splendor, exhibiting the Divine One as ever near to each wanderer, His mighty and majestic heart throbbing mercy and pulsating love—a God who never doubts but that at last He will win man back to rectitude, purity, and divine goodness. For among all the great books of fiction "Les Miserables" is unique, in that it exhibits the worst man as having a divine spark that no injustice can extinguish, a spark which God guards and feeds, making it incorruptible in this life and immortal in the next.

Consider the man who represents the outcasts and stands for the uttermost of suffering and sin as a test of God's power to recover and save. In an era when princes oppressed peasants and plundered them, Jean Valjean was the child of a poor forester. Very early in life he was robbed of his parents, who, stricken with sickness, died from lack of proper food and medicine. Reared by his married sister, when he was seventeen Jean saw her husband lying dead upon a heap of straw, while seven little children, with piteous sobs, clung to their father's dead hands. Then for ten years the boy toiled, as brother, husband, and father, receiving sixteen sous a day for seventeen hours of work. Oft when the children were hungry he bowed his head over his bowl of porridge, that unseen he might slip his piece of bread into the hand of the crying child. Once, when the two little girls went to a neighbor's hut and said their mother wished to buy a quart of milk—milk which they drank to satisfy their cravings—Jean paid the debt to save the children punishment.

For years he rose a great while before day and toiled until long after the darkness fell. In childhood and youth he knew neither teacher nor sweetheart nor friendship. The winter he was twenty-

seven the snow came early, and the cold
was pitiless. Unfortunately, he found himself without work, and daily the children
cried for bread. One night, dumb with their
pain, little Jean, beholding bread in the
baker's window, suddenly struck the glass
with his fist, pulled out a loaf of bread,
and carried it home to the children, that,
satisfied, they might sleep.

The next morning his bleeding arm and
his own confession convicted the youth of
theft. With solemn ceremony, the state
assembled its representatives and proclaimed
a human shipwreck. Having tried him for
burglary and violence, he was condemned to
the galleys for five years. When the judge
bade the soldiers rivet the iron collar about
his neck, an old man who witnessed the
scene said that Jean Valjean sobbed and
moaned, and, lifting his right arm in the
air, lowered it seven times, ever moaning
the names of the seven children whom he
said now must starve. After four years in
the galleys, companying with thieves and
murderers, who seemed to him none other
than human devils, Jean grew desperate and
tried to escape. Caught after long hiding

in a heap of rubbish, three years were added to his sentence. Later, when the attempt to escape was repeated, his sentence was again increased. One day, after nineteen years of imprisonment, he who had gone in sobbing and shuddering came out with a heart as cold as granite and a will as hard as steel.

Often while pounding upon his stone-heap or lying on the convict's plank he had instituted a court of justice, and weighed out judgment and penalty. On the one hand he tried and condemned himself. He freely confessed that children can endure hunger long without dying; that begging bread or borrowing it is better than stealing it; that starving was less than imprisonment, and that in any case sin never halves misfortunes, but only doubles them. But, on the other hand, he asked whether society did not owe something to his sister's orphan children; whether, in view of his twenty-seven years of honest labor, society did not owe him work; whether, when he had confessed his fault to the judge, society had not by its excess of penalty wrought a crime against a citizen, a crime that for nineteen years had been committed afresh daily upon his head. So he tried society, and found it guilty of injustice. He tried Providence, and found Him responsible for his misfortunes. He tried the laws of the state, and found them cruel and unfair, and because he felt that he had reason and justice on his side, his heart was full of fierce indignation. Jean Valjean left the prison knowing that he was cruel, because he felt the wolf's instinct to rend and tear. He knew that he had become bitter, because he made his knife sharp against his fellows. He knew that he was allied to demons, because his heart was full of murderous hate. Can a leopard change his spots? Can a cold marble statue weep? Jean Valjean had not shed a tear for nineteen years! God alone seems equal to that emergency called a bad man's heart.

Over against this convict, injured by his own sins, brutalized by man's injustice, cursed with hatred and consumed with a vain, passionate desire to injure someone, stands the bishop, whom Victor Hugo exhibits as entering the lists to battle with demons for the soul of Jean Valjean. Bun-

yan dreamed his "Great Heart," but Victor
Hugo must have known some pastor of
quality so rare that single-handed he could
sweeten an entire province. The bishop
was generous, and having fifteen thousand
francs annually, he gave fourteen thousand
to the poor. He was a student of books,
but his love for men in trouble amounted to
a passion. He visited the poor so long as
he had money in his pockets, then he visited the rich to fill his purse for further
benefactions. His sympathy was divine.
When a peasant mourned for wife or child,
the good bishop sought him out, and having the art of holding his tongue, sat for
hours without speaking a word to the heartbroken man.

Was a youth overtaken in a sin, he would
say to the magistrate, "We ourselves are
ex-sinners; let us be charitable." When
a man was caught red-handed in a theft,
the bishop said: "Sin is a darkness of
the mind. The state that permitted ignorance and darkness for this youth should
now be sent to jail with the thief." One
day a young man, for love of a girl and her
child, made counterfeit coin. When the

girl was arrested, faithful to her love, she denied that her lover had given her the false money. Then the attorney for the state conceived the plan of provoking her jealousy by declaring her lover had been unfaithful, and exhibiting bits of letters. When she believed her lover recreant to his vows she became desperate, and making a full confession, convicted both the accused man and herself, and so was condemned to death. When the people applauded the attorney's skill, the bishop exclaimed, "This man and woman will go to the scaffold, but who is to hang the state's attorney?"

Once the bishop returned home after a protracted absence. On the following morning a chest was found at his door, within which were a golden cross, a miter rich with gems, a studded crozier, and the royal robes worn by bishops. It was the brigands' present to the priest, who had gone to their camp to plead with them to give up their life of sin. For this bishop is Bunyan's "Great Heart." What kindness to the poor! What tenderness toward the outcast and sinners! What pity for orphans and the fatherless! Little wonder that single-handed the bishop redeemed his diocese to virtue and integrity. Nothing can withstand love's sweet solicitude. Love melts the heart like wax. It warms like sunshine. If oft arguments harden, love can redeem and save.

Unfortunately, when freedom brought a new era, Jean Valjean fell upon other forms of injustice. For his nineteen years of toil he should have received from the state one hundred and seventy-one francs, but, on various pleas, the warden kept back sixty francs. On the morning of his release, dazzled with liberty, Jean made his way to the dock. Finding the workmen were receiving thirty sous a day, he immediately joined the laborers. That night the master paid him fifteen sous, saying, "That is enough for you." When Jean insisted upon his rights, the captain said, "Mind you do not get into prison again." But since society continued to rob him, he now began to hunger for a chance to rob society of something. The next day, consumed with bitterness, Jean started toward his native province. When the darkness of a chill October night fell, he entered a village, only to find that the policeman made him show his yellow ticket, and treated him as though he were less than a man and hardly a beast. Entering an inn, before his supper was ready, something aroused the landlord's suspicion. Finding the stranger had been a convict, he refused Jean food and lodging, and drove him from his door. Learning there was still another inn, Jean called for the landlord and, said, "I am dying of hunger; I have been on my legs since sunrise, and have walked twelve leagues." But a traveler sitting by the fireside made an imperceptible sign, and after a whispered consultation the keeper opened the door and said, roughly, "Be off!"

In his despair the man now made his way to a peasant's house in the edge of the village. Looking through the window, he saw a table spread with white linen, a smoking dish upon the stove, a father laughing at the child upon his knee, and pensively thought that such happiness would surely know pity. Knocking at the door, the man asked why he did not go to this inn and that. Finding that Jean had been refused at both, he suddenly exclaimed, "Can

you be the man?" Then, dropping the
child, he picked up his gun, while the
woman drew her children back, and cried,
"The villain!" After studying Jean as if
he had been a viper, the man exclaimed,
"Be gone!" "For mercy's sake, a glass of
water!" To which the answer was, "Rather
a charge of shot." Going away, he saw
the woman carry food out to the dog in its
kennel, and exclaimed, "And I am not even
a dog!" An hour later, in his despair, he
threw himself down upon the moor. But
the rain-clouds upon the horizon were not
so dark as the black looks that lay upon his
forehead. Suddenly the lightning leaped
from cloud to cloud—strange type of the
hatred that leaped from his heart toward
some one whom it might strike and burn
and wither. Falling upon his knees on the
ground, through very weakness, Jean
looked toward the village, and shook his
clinched fists at the lights of the houses;
shook them at the stars in the sky; cursed
man below, and cursed an unseen One who
dwells above the stars and beyond them.
Dark indeed the hour when man cries,
"No one cares for my soul."

But if landlords were inhospitable, their cruelty was destined to deflect Jean's steps toward the bishop's door. When darkness fell, a neighbor came in to warn the bishop that there was a treacherous character in town, and a moment later there was a loud knock at the door. The man who entered was apparently in middle life, rough, bold, violent, with a fierce and sinister light glowing in his eyes. Standing in the red glow of the fire, his face became hideous. "Look here," he said, in a loud voice, "I am a galley slave. Here is my passport. It reads 'five years for robbery, with housebreaking, and fourteen years for trying to escape four times. The man is very dangerous.' Now will you give me some food and a bed? I can sleep in the stable." The good bishop was kindness itself. "Sit down, sir, and warm yourself. You will sup with us. Afterward your bed will be made ready."

Hardly understanding, Jean began to stammer like a lunatic. Stupefaction, doubt, and joy bewildered his speech. When he urged that he had money, the bishop made him understand that he was a priest, and not a landlord, and said: "You are welcome. This is not my house, but the house of Christ. Your name, sir, was known to me before you gave me your passport. You are my brother." Years later, recalling that hour, Jean remembered that if a moment before he was faint with hunger, the bishop's kindness made his hunger to pass, and that word "sir" was more to him than a cup of water to a shipwrecked sailor. "You have suffered greatly," said the bishop, gently, gazing long into the fire. "Oh! the dogs are happier! Nineteen years! The red jacket, the cannon ball on the foot, a plank to sleep on, heat, cold, labor, blows, the double chain for a nothing, the dungeon for a word, even when you are ill in body, and the chain gang." "A place of sorrow indeed," mused the bishop; "but there is more joy in heaven over one repentant sinner than over the white robes of ninety and nine just men. Ah! sir, if you leave the prison with thoughts of hatred and anger, you are worthy of pity. But if you leave it with thoughts of gentleness and peace toward those who have injured you, you are better than any of us."

After supper, the bishop took one of the silver candlesticks, and handing the other to Jean, led him to his room. But when the convict saw that his bed was next to that of the bishop, he drew back, folded his arms, looked at his host fixedly, and exclaimed: "What! lodge me so close as that! How do you know I am not a murderer?" "That is between you and God," exclaimed the bishop. Then, lifting his hand, he blessed the man, and wishing him good night, turned and left the room.

At midnight that night, startled by the cathedral bells that pealed the hour of two, Jean wakened, dazed by his surroundings. Sitting up, strange, confused thoughts ran wildly through his brain. The thought that was uppermost was that the hour had come for revenge upon society. He had seen the servant put the silver plate into the cupboard near at hand. The soup ladle alone was worth more than he had received for nineteen years of work. Thoughts of liberty, revenge, murder, flight, and wealth chased through his mind, as tiger cubs play in an open glade in a jungle. When the clock struck three he sprang up, pushed

open the bishop's door, and lo! there in the
moonlight lay the aged bishop, his white
hair falling from his noble forehead, his
brow clothed with beauty and majesty as
with garments. Transfixed with terror, Jean
gazed upon that face as upon a vision.
Artists place a halo about their saints, but
in his excited state the convict saw above
the bishop's brow a nimbus of radiant hope
and peace. There was something indescrib-
ably solemn and majestic in the peaceful
sleep of the saintly man. In his agitation
the convict forgot that murder was in his
heart, forgot the club in his hand, forgot
that he had thought to slay his benefactor. Stricken with terror, his teeth
chattered and he grew faint with fear. When
the bishop moved in his sleep, Jean felt the
arteries in his temple beat like two forge
hammers, his breath seemed to issue from
his lungs with the noise of the winds raging
from a cavern, while the hinge turning
sounded like the noise of an earthquake.
When no one roused, his hand released its
grasp upon the crowbar. Turning to flee
from the bishop, as a demon flees from an
angel, the convict saw the case of silver,

and thrusting it under his arm, entered the
garden, leaped over the wall, and fled like
a tiger into the darkness of the night.

But going, he was destined to return.
The morning that brought the breakfast hour
to the bishop brought also five soldiers with
Jean Valjean and the stolen silver. When
the officers entered, the bishop advanced at
once, and stretching out his hand to Jean,
exclaimed: "So you have come back, my
good friend. Here is the rest of your silver.
In giving you the plate I gave you the candlesticks also. They alone will fetch you
two hundred francs." Dismissed, the soldiers went away, and left Jean to the bishop.
The convict trembled in all his limbs, and
the cold sweat stood on his brow. He
looked on the point of fainting. Then the
bishop went to the mantel, fetched the candlesticks and handed them to Jean, who
took them mechanically and with wondering looks. "Never forget that you have
promised me to employ this money in becoming an honest man," said the bishop.
Having no recollection of having promised
anything, Jean Valjean stood silent. Then
the good man stretched forth his hand

and said: "My brother! You no longer belong to evil, but to good. I have bought your soul of you. I withdraw it from black thoughts and the spirit of perdition and give it unto God."

In his great picture, Retzsch shows us angels and demons struggling for the soul of Faust. Oft the demons wing their arrows with flame, but the angels pull roses from the bushes of paradise, and, leaning over the battlements, cast them upon the heads of the combatants. Falling upon the demons, the blossoms turn to coals of fire, but falling upon Faust, they healed his hurts. In that moment when the convict turned from the bishop's door, there was begun a life-and-death struggle for the soul of Jean Valjean. All morning he wandered about the lonely and deserted moor. Jean had eaten nothing, yet he was not hungry. He walked round and round incessantly, yet was not weary. Oft his agitation was such that he wished himself again in his prison cell. Against the softness that now swept over him he set the hardness of twenty years. When a sweetbrier in the hedge reminded him of his mother's garden, his throat choked, and this emotion filled him with new terror. Clinching his fists, he set himself to hold on to the hatred and vengeance that seemed in danger of dissolving.

The falling twilight found him seated under a bush beside the path. By chance a little boy crossing the field saw his dark figure, and with a sharp cry dropped his bundle and a two-franc piece that rolled against the stick of the convict. Thrusting out his foot, Jean covered the coin. When the child asked for his silver, the man sprang up, and lifting his stick, cried out against the little stranger. Not until the boy had fled did Jean realize that he had stolen the coin.

Then the thought that he was a thief went through him like a knife. Unconsciously a change had taken place in him. Victor Hugo tells us he had become incapable of stealing. Forgetting his silver plate, Jean bounded along the path, calling wildly for the child. In vain he looked everywhither. His heart was going like a trip-hammer, his teeth were chattering, though not with the night wind, while the bushes waved their arms like angels of penalty. The light that the good bishop had poured in upon his darkened mind blinded him. His soul seemed like an owl surprised with the excess of light. Conscience whispered that he must either go up beside the bishop and become an angel, or go down beside the demons and become a monster.

So his wickedness and the bishop's goodness griped for their final struggle. In his excitement he thought he saw the bishop's figure lighted up and transfigured before him. Falling upon his knees, he saw that face growing brighter and brighter, while he grew less and less and faded away. At last only the bishop remained, and his smile of approval filled Jean's heart with strange happiness. For a long time he remained upon his knees weeping, with more of emotion than a woman and more of terror than a child. As he wept the light in his brain grew more brilliant. In that light his first sin, his brutalization, his theft of the silver, his hatreds, his purposes of vengeance, seemed monstrous things, and thrust into the white light of the bishop's presence they were utterly consumed away. At last he rose and made his way backward toward the bishop's house. About an hour before daybreak, when the stage-coach for Paris passed through the village, the driver saw a man kneeling on the pavement in the attitude of prayer, with face turned toward the bishop's door. It is Saul, who saw a great light on the way to Damascus. It is David crying, "Create a clean heart in me, O God." It is Peter repenting bitterly of his sin. It is the beautiful girl weeping at the feet of Jesus. It is Christ saying, "Ye may be born again and become as a little child."

It is a proverb that fact is stranger than fiction. Since the history of modern commerce includes the story of a wealthy manufacturer who spent those years included between twenty and forty within the prison walls, but who in later life was renowned as a noble inventor, philanthropist, and reformer, it seems easy to believe that this new era for Jean Valjean's heart, meant also a new era for his intellect. Be the reasons what they may, goodness is medicinal. Peace with one's self and one's God lends the soul wings. If remorse poisons the intellect, the noble impulses fertilize and invigorate the mind. Sin is sand in the soul's wheels, but righteousness is frictionless living. When Jean Valjean rose from the pavement before the bishop's house, he went forth having two thoughts—to "hide his name and sanctify his life, to escape from man and return to God." And not once did he waver from his determination to make himself all that the bishop wished him to be. From the hour when he began life under the new name events conspired to help him. One day he chanced upon a method of making jet from gum lac and turpentine. The change was a revolution. In three years he built two factories; in five years he had a large sum in the bank; in eight years he was known as a philanthropist who had built a hospital for his sick workmen, and founded an industrial school for sick children. He became the almoner of bounty for the widow and the fatherless, made his village in size a little city, and what was better still, made it a veritable hive of industry.

But after eight years, just in the happiest, brightest hour of his new life, there came a moment that was big with peril. One morning he heard that an old man had been

arrested in a neighboring village. It seemed
that this stranger had stolen a bough of
apples. On bringing him to the station, an
official recognized him as a former convict,
one Jean Valjean, who was wanted for stealing a coin from a peasant boy. If the rest
of the day the mayor was "tranquil without,
within there raged a hurricane." He saw
his place at the galleys vacant and this
stranger taking it. Fate seemed to have
found the mayor a substitute. For years he
had longed and prayed for one thing—se-
curity. And now that Javert had this
Jean Valjean in his clutches, the mayor
might have rest and peace. Once the old
man was convicted under his name, Jean
Valjean was dead. In that hour of temptation "God heaved the soul like an ocean."
Suddenly the very thought of allowing that
innocent man to be condemned in his stead
stood forth a low and hideous crime. Not
to confess himself as Jean Valjean was to
thrust this stranger into the galleys and to
assassinate his life. While the tempest raged
in his brain, the figure of the bishop rose before him, and a voice whispered: "If the
bishop were here he would have you go to

Arras and deliver the false Jean Valjean and denounce the true one." Yet when his resolve to confess his identity was made, the temptation began afresh. To surrender himself was to give up his factory, and desert his poor villagers, who depended upon his industry. He remembered that it was his skill that had lighted the fires in the factory and placed the meat in the pot. Also when industry had driven out poverty, the mendicancy, vice, and crime had passed also. Suddenly something whispered, "Events have decided." Then he arose, and unlocked the secret cabinet. He took the silver candlesticks, his old knapsack and stick, and hurling all into the fire, destroyed the last thing that connected him with Jean Valjean, and left the stranger to his fate. Suddenly some one seemed to pronounce his name in a whisper that fell from above. Then terror overtook him. His hair stood erect. The perspiration beaded his forehead. He heard a sound of demoniac laughter ringing through the chambers of his heart, as if demons were laughing at the conquest of man's soul. Should he remain in that paradise named the mayor's house, and by remaining become a demon, or should he go back to that hell, the galleys, that he might be an angel there? And so he writhed in his agony until at last, with blood upon his lips, he knelt and breathed this prayer: "Not my will but Thine be done." Staggering within and without, he received the cup of pain, as eighteen hundred years before "that mysterious being in whom all the sanctities and suffering were united, met His Gethsemane."

Literature holds no more thrilling chapter than the story of the mayor entering the dock to assume the convict's garb. For the very next day M. Madeleine ascended the bench beside the judge, and bade the jury acquit the prisoner. When the magistrate thought him crazed with trouble, and wondered, doubting, Mayor Madeleine called the names of the two convicts who had been brought from the prison to identify the old man. He told one that he had two letters burned upon his right shoulder; he told the other that in the hollow of his left arm was a date made in blue letters with burnt gunpowder. When the soldiers found these marks, and the men knew that the mayor was indeed Jean Valjean, the judge and the people felt a great light shining in the room, and were "dazzled in their hearts." Divine and majestic indeed the man who could denounce himself lest another be condemned in his place. Hath God transformed a convict into a savior? "Greater love hath no man than this, that a man lay down his life," not "for his friends," but for his enemies. But to the audience full of tears and pity Jean Valjean said: "You consider me worthy of pity. Great God! When I think of what I was on the point of doing I consider myself worthy of envy." And so, obedient to the heavenly vision, Jean turned again toward the Inferno, above whose door these words were written, "Abandon hope all ye who enter here."

Then began a new series of struggles, more thrilling than Bunyan's story of Christian's fight with Apollyon. Condemned afresh, Jean escapes from his prison. Having saved himself, he remembers the dying charge of Fantine, and rescues little Cosette from the beast that was misusing her. Putting the child in a school, he hid himself near a convent, and out of his apparent poverty became the almoner of bounty to the weak and poor. And as the years went on, he who had never known the love of mother or sweetheart or wife, poured the vast treasures of his love about the orphan child that he had made to be his daughter. In love's sweet atmosphere his very life did blossom. Ever ministering to God's poor, Jean's life was full of sweetness and happiness. But when ten years had passed, events startled him. He beheld his tall and beautiful daughter possessed of dreams of love and home. Grievous indeed was the shock. Should Cosette leave him, for fear of discovery he could never enter her home. Her going meant the snuffing out of the candle of his happiness. Henceforth his days must be darkness. He who could thrust a hot iron into his hand and endure the burning flesh without flinching felt his soul passing into the crucible. At the moment when the temptation was fiercest, he learned that his daughter's lover was in a position of extreme peril, and that unless he hastened forth for rescue the youth must perish, leaving him in peace with the one whom he loved. In that hour the voice of conscience, that he now knew to be the voice of Christ, whispered, "He saved others, Himself he cannot save." So he went forth again into the darkness and the storm. One day, at the risk of his own life, he saved the life of Marius, and gave his daughter into her lover's arms. He who had redeemed others out of death to life, now became a martyr and mounted his scaffold.

Then events moved swiftly on toward the end of the piteous tragedy. One day he saw his daughter cross the threshold of a beauteous home, and when the door closed he stood in the darkness without, and knew that he was in the night and cold forevermore. One sacrifice remained. He could live meanly, in poverty. His daughter needed wealth and a dowry. So Jean Valjean emptied his entire fortune into his daughter's hands, saying that he had held it in trust against her marriage day. When Marius, not knowing that Jean was the Mayor Madeleine, suspected him of having slain the manufacturer and stolen his wealth, Valjean hid himself in a garret in a distant part of the city, and denied himself the feast of beholding his daughter's face. But God is just. At last every wrong is righted. The day came when son and daughter knew that, being rich, Jean Valjean had made himself poor that they might have home and happiness. Marius knew that he had given treachery, suspicion, and ingratitude to the man who had saved his life. Cosette knew that having neither name nor home nor friends, that one whom she had neglected had lent her patrician place and luxury and happiness. Javert knew that he had been a wolf joining the pack to chase down a noble stag.

Realizing that this man was possessed of every virtue; that his was the heroism of Savonarola to accept flame; his the strength of Socrates to receive the poison cup; his the fortitude of Paul to endure the whips and scourge of "outrageous fortune," this son and daughter hastened forth to find his garret. Falling on their knees beside the dying man, they besought his forgiveness and confessed their selfishness and shameful ingratitude. In the hour of death the hero, worn with suffering and scarred with many wounds received in noble battle, laid his hands upon their heads and said: "My children, remember God is above. He sees all. He knows all He does, amid His great stars. Remember God is love." Pointing to the crucifix, he whispered, "There is the Great Martyr." Then silence fell upon the weeping group. While their hot tears fell upon his hand, they looked up and found Jean Valjean looking into the open heavens, with a great, sweet smile upon his face. "My children, I can no longer see very clearly. I had several things to say to you, but no matter. Think of me a little. I know not what is the matter with me, but *I see light*." Then the long silence startled the weeping son and daughter. The night was starless and intensely dark; doubtless some angel was standing in the gloom, with outstretched hands, waiting for the soul. God and His angels had conquered in the long battle for the city of man's soul.

VI

Tennyson's "Idylls of the King"—An Outlook upon the Soul's Epochs and Teachers

But when we take the King and his people as actual men and women, when we throw ourselves into the story and let it carry us along, then we understand that it is a parable; that is to say, it "throws beside" itself an image, a reflection, of something spiritual, just as a man walking in the sunlight is followed by his shadow. It is a tale of human life, and therefore, being told with a purpose, it

Shadows sense at war with soul.

Arthur is intended to be a man in whom the spirit has already conquered and reigns supreme. It is upon this that his kingship rests. His task is to bring his realm into harmony with himself, to build up a spiritual and social order upon which his own character, as the best and highest, shall be impressed. In other words, he works for the uplifting and purification of humanity. It is the problem of civilization. His great enemies in this task are not outward and visible —the heathen—for these he overcomes and expels. But the real foes that oppose him to the end are the evil passions in the hearts of men and women about him. So long as these exist and dominate human lives, the dream of a perfected society must remain unrealized; and when they get the upper hand, even its beginnings will be destroyed. But the conflict is not an airy, abstract strife; it lies in the opposition between those in whom the sensual principle is regnant and those in whom the spiritual principle is regnant, and in the inward struggle of the noble heart against evil, and of the sinful heart against the good. —*The Poetry of Tennyson, pp. 177, 178.*

VI

TENNYSON'S "IDYLLS OF THE KING"—AN OUTLOOK UPON THE SOUL'S EPOCHS AND TEACHERS

The year 1809 may well be called *annus mirabilis* for the English-speaking people. That year gave birth to four of the greatest men of the century: Lincoln the emancipator, Darwin the scientist, Gladstone the statesman, and Tennyson the poet. The martyred president gave a new liberty to slaves, the English scientist stands for a new principle in philosophy, the great statesman for a new idea in politics, while the poet led our generation from doubt back to faith. If the influence of president, prime minister, and philosopher has been more dramatic and imposing, that of the poet has been not less powerful and permanent. If Lincoln destroyed bondage for slaves, Tennyson lent meaning to the new liberty. If Gladstone gave the suffrage to classes hitherto disfranchised, the poet lent men the manhood that justified the suffrage. If Darwin gave a new method to the intellect, Tennyson lent new treasure to the heart and conscience. Passing by the soldier, the philosopher, and the king, God hath given the poet in every age the first place in the affections of the people. That which theologians cannot do, the poets easily accomplish. From David's far-off era down to the time of Browning and Tennyson, God hath breathed into poems and songs the revelation of His providence and His love.

Turretin stands for a full hundred men famed as philosophers and theologians, but men have quite forgotton their dogmatics. Bunyan was an untaught tinker, who wrote a dream of the pilgrim's progress heavenward, yet his poetic fire still burns and his pilgrim "holds on his way as strong and fresh as ever." "Not until we know why the rose is sweet, the dewdrop pure, or the rainbow beautiful," said Curtis, "will we know why the poet is the best benefactor of society; but certain it is that he is the divinely ordained teacher, harmonizer, and consoler." To our doubting and bewildered generation Tennyson seems like some glorious Hebrew sage or seer returned to earth to lead men into paths of light and peace. Unfortunately for his time, Shelley led a blind revolt from all forms of belief. Arthur Hugh Clough followed, but he stood hesitant midway between doubt and faith, and soon lost his leadership. Becoming pessimistic, Matthew Arnold struck the note of "eternal sadness." But Tennyson bravely faced the specters of the mind. He fought his doubts and gathered strength, and after long groping in the darkness emerged into a blaze of light. "At last he beat his music out," and sang the deep, wide love of God, the deathless destiny of man, the radiant beauty and perfection of Christ as the soul's savior. His "In Memoriam" is the most important religious poem of the century. His songs called "Doubt and Prayer," "God and His Universe," "The Silent Voices," "Crossing the Bar," were his last will and testament to the world. Of Tennyson it may be said, as it was of Cromwell, "He was a strong man in the dark perils of war, and in the high places of the field hope shone in him like a pillar of fire when it had gone out in others.''

For our literary critics it is not enough to mention Tennyson as the most representative poet of the Victorian era, ''The God-gifted organ voice of England who hath written lyrics which must charm all who love, epics which must move all who act, songs that must cheer all who suffer, poems which must fascinate all who think.'' Great as he was as a poet, Tennyson was greater still as a man and a Christian. What leader has made so profound an impression upon his fellows or won such tribute of praise from the great men of his time! One day grim Thomas Carlyle met Tennyson and went away to write of him: ''One of the finest men in the world. A great shock of rough, dusky-dark hair; bright, laughing hazel eyes; massive, aquiline face, most massive, yet most delicate; sallow brown complexion, almost Indian-looking; clothes cynically loose, free and easy; smokes infinite tobacco. His voice is musically metallic, fit for loud laughter and piercing wail and all that might lie between.''

No man of his era was so swift in piercing

through disguises as Thackeray, yet he called Tennyson "one of the wisest of men." Gladstone had a great conception of the poet as a philosopher. "I look upon him in his words and works with reverence. The sage of Chelsea was a genius small in comparison with Tennyson." Lord Shelburne called him "the foremost man of his generation. He realized to me more than any one else whom I have known the heroic idea." Upon the occasion of his last illness, Tennyson looked up into the face of one who was standing by him and said, "I should be sorely afraid to live my life without God's presence, but to feel that He is by my side now, just as much as you are, that is the very joy of my heart." But he who went toward death with the faith of God strengthening his heart went through life with the light of God shining upon his face. Recalling a week in the poet's home, a gifted friend who knew him best wrote, "Talking with Alfred Tennyson seemed to lift me out of the earth—earthy. It was like what a retreat is to the religious." For precious as are his poems, Tennyson's character and career are treasures beyond all the achievements of his splendid intellect. Like his own King Arthur, he wore "the white flower of a blameless life." Like Milton he daily pledged himself to conscience and his God, "believing that he who would write well in laudable things ought himself to be a true poem," and therefore hoped "to leave something so written that men should not willingly let it die."

In his memoirs of the poet laureate, Hallam Tennyson tells us that his father left his last religious poem as a final message to the world, "summing up the faith in which he had lived." Fascinating indeed the story how Tennyson moved from doubt to belief. It happened that the young poet entered the university at a moment when doubt was becoming a fad and faith a form of folly. The era of his manhood was by way of preëminence the era of skepticism. Carrying their principle to a rash extreme, some evolutionists rose up to say that the brain secretes thought, as the liver secretes bile. These writers also explained the optimism of one philosopher and the pessimism of another by the shifting of the brain molecules. They accounted for the supreme enthusiasm and victory of Socrates and Savonarola by the pressure of gases upon the arteries of the brain. The magician in the "Arabian Nights" waved his wand above an empty jug, and from the mouth thereof evoked an orange seed that swelled, waxed into a tree, put forth its buds, ripened the golden fruit, while another wave of the wand caused the tree to retreat into seed and jug—and all this marvel, too, in a moment of time. But this wonder tale seems as nothing compared to the feats that the philosopher could produce with that magician named "matter." One molecule and a little moisture—these were sufficient to account for an "Iliad," a "Principia," a St. Paul's Cathedral. In that era of sneers and paralyzing doubts, full many a gifted boy in England's university made shipwreck of his faith. Even Arthur Hugh Clough, with his rare intellect and deep religious nature, was bewildered, and became, as Thomas Arnold said, "the Hamlet of the nineteenth century." In such an atmosphere Tennyson passed his youth and maturity. He was a brave doubter, and was familiar with every attack that could be made upon Christ and Christianity. Becoming increasingly interested in nature and science, he fronted every form of materialism and agnosticism with every ideal substitute for God. Among his closest friends were Huxley and Tyndall, and by years of study he became almost a specialist in the principles of physics and biology. Later, Professor Norman Lockyer tells us he turned to astronomy and saturated his mind with the facts of that fascinating science. In saying to Charles Darwin, "Your theory of evolution does not make against Christianity," to which Darwin answered, "Certainly not," Tennyson does but express the conclusion to which he himself had arrived after long investigation.

> He fought his doubts and gathered strength,
> He would not make his judgment blind.
> He faced the specters of the mind
> And laid them; thus he came at length
> To find a stronger faith than was his own.

Of God he said: "Take away belief in the self-conscious personality of God and you take away the backbone of the world. I should infinitely rather feel myself the most miserable wretch on the face of the earth, with a God above, than the highest type of man standing alone. My most passionate desire is for a clearer and fuller vision of God." Not less clear were his convictions about Christ. "Christianity, without the central figure of the Son of Man, becomes cold. I am amazed at the splendor of Christ's purity and holiness and at His infinite beauty." If he disliked discussion as to the nature of Christ, because "none knoweth the Son but the Father," he affirmed that Christ was "the Maker, the Lord, the Light, the Life indeed." Of prayer he said that it was like opening "a sluice between the great ocean and our little channels when the sea gathers itself together and flows in at full tide." "More things are wrought by prayer than this world dreams of—

" For what are men better than sheep or goats,
That nourish a blind life within the brain,
If, knowing God, they lift not hands of prayer
Both for themselves and those who call them friends?
For so the whole round earth is every way
Bound by gold chains about the feet of God."

In no great author has the faith of immortality been more deep and strong. "I can hardly understand," said Tennyson, "how any great imaginative man who has deeply lived, suffered, thought, and wrought can doubt of the soul's continuous progress in after life.'' For one by one Tennyson conquered his doubts, and at last those faiths called God, Christ, prayer, sin, repentance, forgiveness, immortality, became for him faiths as immovable as the mountains, as permanent as the stars that guide the mariner homeward.

From one view-point Tennyson's ''In Memoriam'' is the most important religious poem of the century, but from another ''The Idylls of the King'' forms a moral parable of equal value and importance. Because they represent the maturity of his genius and the perfection of his art, his deepest convictions and his highest wisdom, the ''Idylls'' would seem to form the poem upon which his fame must ultimately rest. The works of Tennyson include more than three hundred quotations from the Bible, and are pervaded with a spirit so deeply devout that men have come to feel that he is essentially our religious poet, and that it is in the realm of religious thought that his genius has found its highest expression. If the "Paradise Lost" looks backward and shows how one sin sent one man into the wilderness; if the "Divine Comedy" looks forward and shows how sins may be punished and purged away, "The Idylls of the King" forms a study of the present and offers an outlook upon the great epochs and teachers of the soul.

Interpreting his own poem, Tennyson says: "Birth is a mystery and death is a mystery, and midway between lies the table-land of life with its struggles and perplexities." For David, man comes made in God's image; for Wordsworth, man comes "trailing clouds of glory"; for Tennyson, "man comes from the great deep, to the great deep he goes." Arthur stands out as a mystic incarnation, a Christ-man, pure, noble, unerring. He is the perfect flower of purity and chivalry. He wars against Lancelot as the spirit against the flesh. The fall of his Round Table is the fall of the city of man's soul. The tragedy of King Arthur's career is that man struggles for the highest things for himself and others, only to find his work undone through the weakness and folly of his followers. Recalling the pledges that Christ asks from His disciples, Tennyson represents the knights of the Round Table as laying their hands in King Arthur's while they swear:

> To reverence their conscience as their king,
> To break the heathen and uphold the Christ,
> To ride abroad redressing human wrongs,
> To speak no slander, no, nor listen to it,
> To honor his own words as if his God's,
> To lead sweet lives in purest chastity,
> To love one maiden only, cleave to her,
> To worship her by years of noble deeds,
> Not only to keep down the base in man,
> But teach high thought and amiable words
> And courtliness and the desire of fame
> And love of truth and all that makes a man.

And this mystic king, half-human, half-divine, hath such purity that when his knights lay hands in his, into their faces comes "a momentary likeness of the king." For Arthur stands for man's soul, made in the image of God and clothed with power to redeem and save its fellows.

In his "Gareth and Lynette" Tennyson tells us man's growth begins with struggle, testing, and discipline, and that character is not so much protected innocence as practiced virtue. Gareth is a youth, nobly born, and the very incarnation of ambition, honor, purity, and aspiration. To this boy, living in his mother's castle, surrounded by servants who fetch and carry for him, comes the vision of a fair life he has never led, and forth he goes, preferring to be vanquished in the right to being victorious in the wrong. Refused a commission as knight by reason of his youth, he becomes a scullion in Arthur's kitchen if only he may be near to this glorious king. When Lynette, fleeing from her enemies, seeks refuge in Arthur's castle, Gareth undertakes the dangerous task of freeing her land from enemies. Going forth without fear, the boy is unconquerable, because he knows not when he has been conquered. Fighting against four knights, he unhorses all. Falling into an ambush, he escapes unscathed. When the night fell, and he was worn with the heat and burden of the day, Gareth is again victorious, like one who, having slain the sins of his youth and his maturity, slays also the sins of his old age. For, slowly rising on stepping-stones of his dead self, Gareth climbs to higher things. If, conscious of his kingly birth, he suffers because Lynette counts him a scullion and treats him with

contempt, finally his bravery dissolves her
scorn, compels her admiration, and wins her
love.   At last he rides forth against the
knight of the Black Armor named Death.
When Death's helmet is cloven by Gareth,
forth leaped the bright face of a blooming
boy, "fresh as a new-born flower," and
Gareth, conquering Death, wins an immortal
youth.   What would Tennyson have us
understand from this idyll of Gareth?   It is
Plato saying, "Temptation is the first
teacher."   It is Emerson saying, "The
youth who surrenders himself to a great
ideal himself becomes great."   It is Stop-
ford Brooke saying, "The soul that laughs
and loves and rides for the right has all the
world at his feet."   It is Ruskin saying,
"To be heroic is happiness; to bear all
bravely and righteously in the dazzling sunshine of the morning; not to forget God,
in whom you trust, when He gives you
most; not to forget those who trust you
when they seem to need you least—this is
the difficult fortitude."   It is Sir Galahad
himself, "whose strength is the strength of
ten, because his heart is pure."   It is God
making invincible the arm of the young

knight errant, who will lose his life to save his ideals and save his fellows.

In the Geraint and Enid there is a rift in the lute that will make the music dumb. In this idyll we see how one sin can mar the soul, making the days bitterness and the nights anguish. Like Saul, Geraint was a goodly youth. Like David, he vanquished an enemy in an unequal combat. Like Othello, he met his wife's loyalty and devotion with suspicion and jealous exaction. Doubting the queen's honor, he who has brought Enid to her court drags her forth into the wilderness. Waking one morn, he finds his wife weeping, and concludes that she is false. If jealousy has made Geraint's lips dumb, love makes Enid unwilling to defend herself. Thinking only of himself, the king rides forth into the forest, compelling Enid to go on before, so that she is the first to encounter danger. Although forbidden to speak to her lord, she braves his anger to warn him of enemies lying in ambush. Left alone with rude brigands, her purity and her blazing eyes hold the bandits at bay. In an hour when she believed her husband dead, her devotion and courage rose to a supreme height. She stands forth like an angel of loveliness, clothed with devotion, patience, and purity. At last her beautiful spirit shames Geraint's doubt, dissolves his jealousy, recovers him to the sanity of trust and love. And when the sin is put away, the cloud passes from the sky.

> And never yet, since high in paradise
> O'er the four rivers the first roses blew,
> Came purer pleasure unto mortal kind,
> Than lived through her who in that perilous hour
> Put hand to hand beneath her husband's heart
> And felt him hers again; she did not weep,
> But o'er her meek eyes came a happy mist
> Like that which kept the heart of Eden green
> Before the useful trouble of the rain.

Then for Arthur's court the sin that at first had been so small became a contagion that polluted all the air. Even those who stood upon the outermost circle of Lancelot's life felt the shadow of his black deed. One youth of the Round Table was there, named Balin. In childhood he learned ungovernable anger from his father. In manhood oft his anger raged like an inner demon. But Arthur was patient toward the young knight, who had his repentant moods, and slowly taught Balin courtesy and gentleness. Two ideals the young knight cherished. He looked to Lancelot as unto earth's bravest knight. He looked toward Guinevere as toward earth's noblest lady. What a shock was his when first he learned of the queen's falsity and the knight's faithlessness! In that moment perished Balin's faith in every form of good. Thenceforth his hand was against every man. One day, warring with a stranger, he turned his weapons against his own brother, and slaying him, received his mortal wound. So the death of the two brave knights lay at the door of these guilty ones who had wrecked the faith of a youth bravely struggling upward. Having sent forth a shower of sparks, the great engine speeds on, but the spark falling into the grass, where it kindles a conflagration, is one with the flame in the engine that now hath journeyed afar. And man is responsible for his unconscious influence, that is remote and from which he hath journeyed afar, not less than for the deeds just at hand.

In the Merlin and Vivien, sins that once were secret become bold and impudent. Vivien is the very queen of wickedness.

Ascending her throne, with notes of defiance she publishes the sin of the guilty knight. Beautiful without, she was all black within. Creeping through the court, she spread the scandal regarding Guinevere. She laughs at the folly of those knights who refused to stretch forth the hand and pluck life's scarlet blossoms. Delilah-like, she cast her spell on Merlin, that Samson of intellect, and spoiled him of his strength. Spreading more and more, sin soils all, save Arthur, Sir Bors, Galahad, Percival, and his sister. Tempted in her hours of luxury and leisure, the beautiful Ettarre proves false to her sworn pledge, and is slain for her faithlessness. Wounded by the treachery of his bosom friend, maddened by the falsehood of one whom he loves as life itself, Pelleas rushes into the darkness and the storm, and falls on death. But if this noble youth is ruined by the perfidy of a wicked world, Tristram suffers a deeper hurt. In him sin has made the light to be darkness. He follows that false fire, the will-o'-the-wisp, kindled by passion. Brutalized by wickedness and sodden in sin, his delicacy at last dies. With flippant, jaunty air he talks of the freedom of loving where one wills, and how affection fails when beauty fails. Then, overtaken red-handed in his sins, the avenger smites him unto death. For what man sows, that he reaps.

And when sin and selfishness have wrought havoc in the soul, love comes in to bless when pure, to blight when unholy. What fire is to an opal, that love is to man's life. Wisdom can inform man, but love alone can mellow and mature him. Therefore great authors make the hero's supremacy to begin with the beginning of love. Laura lends purity to Petrarch. Beatrice lends light to Dante. Highland Mary lends music to Burns. Elizabeth Barrett lends maturity to Robert Browning. Men go through years without fulfilling the growth and happiness of a day. Then suddenly the beloved one stands forth, and lo! the horizons take wings and flee away, new worlds swing solemnly into sight; love smites "the chords of self, that, trembling into music, pass from sight." Then the sacrifice becomes a joy, service is a sacrament, devotion is delight. But love is a flame that must be fed by answering love, and, met with dishonor, the loving heart doth break.

The Maid of Astolat is the very lily of womanhood. The queen is a spiced rose of rich perfumes and opulent petals. When the wounded knight came to her father's castle, Elaine served, sacrificed, revered, worshiped, loved in a sweet abandon of trust. And when Lancelot, healed by her medicines, kissed her, offered friendship, and dropped dark hints of his sad story, earth's rude winds and harsh wickedness broke Elaine's pure, innocent spirit. Midway between this daughter of love and purity and this queen whose beauty had rich scarlet and gold and black mingled with its whiteness, stood Lancelot, who might have been the noblest of all the knights, whose tragedy it is that he would fain be loyal to his king without being disloyal to his queen. Yet fidelity to Arthur bade him flee from the court, and fidelity to Guinevere made him false to King Arthur.

Therefore his honor in this honor stood,
And his faith unfaithful kept him falsely true.

At last sin's black cloud bursts into full storm. Lancelot flees. Dumb with pain and stunned with anguish, the knights move through the Round Table like white ghosts. Then war breaks forth. Burning villages light up the plains. Twelve great battles, "sword and fire, red ruin, the breaking up of laws"—these were the doom of Arthur and the fruit of Lancelot's sin. Not until long time had passed was the king victorious over his black and ruined land.

Foreseeing the end of his career, one question ever fronted this flower of knights: Must this separation from Guinevere be eternal? Is there no place of recovery for this daughter of beauty? Is there no hope for the fallen, and no life for the lost? The prodigal found welcome in his father's house, and perchance there is recovery for this queen, weeping in the monastery, where for months she hath hidden. Bitter! oh how bitter her prayers!

" Late, late, so late! and dark the night and chill;
  Late, late, so late, but we can enter still.
  Too late, too late, ye cannot enter now.
  Have we not heard, the bridegroom is so sweet?
  O, let us in, though late to kiss his feet.
  No, no; too late; ye cannot enter now."

That night in the darkness the king sat on horseback at the door.

> And near him the sad nuns, with each a light,
> Stood, and he gave them charge about the queen,
> To guard and foster her forevermore.
> She did not see his face,
> Which then was as an angel's, but she saw
> The vapor rolling round the king
> Enwound him fold by fold, and made him gray
> And grayer, till himself became as mist before her
> Moving ghostlike to his doom.

O, wondrous transformation! Wakening from the awful dream of sin, she became a horror to herself. In that moment, conscious of great love for the injured king, repentance swept over her like the billows of the sea.

> Now I see thee, what thou art!
> Thou art the highest and most human, too;
> Not Launcelot, nor another!
> Is there none will tell the king I love him, though
>   so late,
> Now—ere he goes to that great battle? None.
> Myself must tell him in that purer life,
> But now it were too daring.

Sacrificial love hath redeemed the soul from sin. Forgiven, she pours her life into good deeds, and when years have passed, abbess, as once she had been queen, she passed to "where beyond these voices there is peace."

Then sounds the note of final victory. Adversity, war, ingratitude, the faithlessness of friends within, the hatred of enemies without—all these had conspired to break the king's spirit. But, rising triumphant over every enemy, this flower of kings, this knightliest of all brave men, snatches faith from faithlessness, keeps love midst hate, meets dishonor with forgiveness. When the last battle has been fought, and friends and enemies lie together upon the field, and the Round Table hath fallen, and the great king passes toward death, the valiant knight Sir Bors breaks down and cries:

> Ah, my Lord Arthur! Whither shall I go?
> Where shall I hide my forehead and my eyes?
> For now I see the true old times are dead.

But, clothed with confidence, majesty, and beauty, King Arthur answers that death does not end all.

> The old order changes, yielding place to new,
> And God fulfills Himself in many ways,
> Lest one good custom should corrupt the world;
> By prayer the whole round earth is every way
> Bound by gold chains about the feet of God.

Then passing into the barge, where the
three queens wait to give him guidance and
convoy homeward, he who "came from the
great deep to the great deep was gone."
And the knight, fallen on his knees and
listening, heard sounds—

> As if some fair city were one voice,
> Around a king returning from his wars.

Though our libraries include the books of
earth's most gifted children, yet no great
book or author better illustrates the principle that the great poet must first of all be
a great man. What Tennyson wrote, he
first was. As those knights by looking
into King Arthur's face borrowed a momentary likeness of their king, so Tennyson,
lingering long before his divine Master, borrowed the likeness of that strong Son of
God of whom he sang. Grandly beautiful
the closing hours of his illustrious career!
The dying poet opened his Shakespeare to
those tender lines in "Cymbeline," "Hang
thou like fruit, my soul, till the tree dies."
Talking to his physician about death, he
exclaimed, "What shadows this life is, and
how men cling to what is, after all, but a
small part of the great world's life."

Knowing of the poet's interest in the lot of lowly men, the physician told him of a villager ninety years old who had so pined to see his invalid wife that they carried her to his bedside. "Come soon," said the old man, and soon after passed away himself. The poet murmured, "True faith," and then himself sank into death's sleep. Striking indeed the son's account of that dying scene: "On the bed a figure of breathing marble, flooded and bathed in the light of the full moon streaming through the oriel window; the moonlight, the majestic figure as he lay there, drawing thicker breath, irresistibly brought to our minds his own 'Passing of Arthur.' And when the poet breathed his last, the old pastor, with raised hands, said, 'Truly, Lord Tennyson, God hath taken you, who made you a prince of men.'"

VII

A Study of Browning's "Saul" — The Tragedy of the Ten-Talent Men and their Recovery

                          " To make such a soul,

Such a body, and then such an earth for insphering
    the whole?

And doth it not enter my mind (as my warm tears
    attest)

These good things being given, to go on, and give
    one more, the best?

Ay, to save and redeem and restore him, maintain
    at the height

This perfection, — succeed with life's dayspring,
    death's minute of night?

Interpose at the difficult minute, snatch Saul the
    mistake,

Saul the failure, the ruin he seems now,—and bid
    him awake

From the dream, the probation, the prelude, to find
    himself set

Clear and safe in new light and new life,—a new
    harmony yet

To be run, and continued, and ended—who knows?
    —or endure!

The man taught enough, by life's dream, of the rest
    to make sure;

By the pain-throb, triumphantly winning intensified
    bliss,

And the next world's reward and repose, by the
    struggles of this."

—Poetical Works of Robert Browning,
Vol. III, pp. 120, 121

VII

A STUDY OF BROWNING'S "SAUL"—THE
   TRAGEDY OF THE TEN-TALENT MEN
   AND THEIR RECOVERY

For divers reasons the tragedy of Saul
seems to have fascinated the thought of our
greatest poets, dramatists, and musicians.
In pitying admiration, Browning in his
poem, Stanley in his story, and Chopin in
his "Funeral March," have enshrined the
young king in a mausoleum nobler than one
built of marble. With a certain mournful
awe these admirers watch this richly gifted
youth moving from the summit of greatness
and power down to his wreckage and final
ruin. Romantic indeed this adventurous
and many-colored career that began with
the shepherd's cot, passed swiftly to the
king's palace, and ended midst the shock
and thunder of battle! A born king and
leader among men, he enters the scene
clothed with that irresistible fascination that
only the greatest possess. Like Agamem-

non, he was a king who stood head and shoulders above his people. Like Theseus, he was a soldier whose sword was in his hand by day, whose spear touched his pillow by night. Like Napoleon, with his old guard, about young Saul there stood a band of noble youths of brave beauty and brawny stature. If Lancelot, the leader of King Arthur's knights, lost his leadership through treachery to friendship, Saul also discrowned himself because he was a king untrue to his people, a soldier false to the chivalry of arms, a friend who betrayed his friend. Crowned king at a time when one swift blow would have scattered his foes and united his friends, like Hamlet, Saul stood midway between his duty and his task, and indecision slew him.

Watching this fascinating human figure, with all its splendid gifts, moving swiftly from virtue to vice, from the palace to the slave market, until his faculties are all entangled and confused, oft does the heart long, but long in vain, to hear "the exulting and triumphant cry of a strong man coming to himself and saying, 'I will arise.'"

Pathetic indeed the story of his decline

and fall. When pride had engendered selfishness, vanity brought in jealousy. One day, after young David had vanquished the boasted champion of an invading army, the hero's appearance in the street was greeted with the cheers and exultant shouts of the multitude. In that hour King Saul feared a shepherd boy, and hurling his javelin at the youth, met the contempt of all brave men. But as the sun disappears when the eye is blind, so Saul tampered with his conscience, until, for this fallen king, God was as though He were not. Like a mariner who has lost both sun and compass, bewildered, Saul turned toward a fortune-teller, who pondered the leaves in the bottom of a cup, and studied beads and amulets for a great man's guidance. Soon this prince, who in his strength had planned the movements of an army, asked a wandering gypsy to determine the path in which his faltering feet and shattered intellect should walk. Therefore, when the piteous tragedy ended, men cried out, "How are the mighty fallen!" Sad, indeed, the ruin of this great king! It is some monarch of the forest rearing its lofty branches high above the far-reaching woods, to be stricken by the thunderbolt and left black and scarred and ruined. It is the Parthenon, once crowned with matchless beauty, become a mere shell of its former self, a heap, and desolation. It is some great ship, falling upon cruel rocks that gore its sides, while from the yeasty, spray-darkened beach there rises the bitter cry, "A wreck, a wreck!" When men bore the body of the king into the market-place, they wept indeed, but not because Saul had been overtaken by death. Their hot tears fell because they remembered the brave boy, once so pure and stainless and true, who had made his career to be, not a triumph, but a tragedy; whose soul at last seemed like a palace devastated by fire, like a rich harvest field, where the tornado had made wide its path of ruin!

The saddest chapter in literature is the history of our ten-talent men. Lingering long upon the career of these sons of genius, we turn from their dark story with the reflection that often greatness seems to be a menace, prosperity a peril, and position a test and strain. The scholars of Venice tell us that the "mistress of the sea" had her vast treasures, not through a few great ships, but by a multitude of lesser vessels. And ours is a world where the richest cargoes of the soul sweep forward in fleets made up of those lesser craft named "two-talent people." What great men cannot do, average men easily achieve. A few elect ones there are who seem like vast ships laden with treasures, upon whose decks stand the harpers with their harps, but at whose helms there are no pilots, and oft the galleon has gone down in sight of the harbor where the smaller craft have peacefully landed their treasures and received welcome and victory.

In that fascinating study called "The Makers of Modern English" the first six chapters tell the story of six sons of genius and greatness. Strangely enough, the career of four of these richly dowered men was a tragedy, that of Keats an unfulfilled prophecy, while that of Scott alone was an unmarred triumph. Here is Burns, of whom Carlyle asks: "Will a courser of the sun work softly in the harness of a trade horse? His hoofs are of fire, his path is in the heavens, his task bringing light to all lands.

Will he lumber over mud roads, dragging ale for earthly appetites from door to door?'' Yet such a tragedy was the life of Burns! He was the child of supreme genius. After a century his songs are still the richest treasure of a nation that has immeasurable wealth. Himself a song-intoxicated man, with melody he hath bewitched all peoples. Striking a new note in English literature, this fresh, buoyant, impassioned singer enters the scene like an ethereal visitor from some celestial realm. Of his amazing intellect, Walter Scott said Burns had condensed the essence of a thousand novels in these four lines:

> Had we never loved so blindly,
> Had we never loved so kindly,
> Never met and never parted,
> We had ne'er been broken-hearted.

What Raphael is in color, what Mozart is in music, that Burns is in song. With his sweet words "the mother soothes her child, the lover wooes his bride, the soldier wins his victory." His biographer says his genius was so overmastering that the news of Burns's arrival at the village inn drew farmers from their fields, and at midnight

wakened travelers, who left their beds to
listen, delighted, until the morn.

One day this child of poverty and obscurity left his plow behind, and entering the
drawing-rooms of Edinburgh, met Scotland's most gifted scholars, her noblest
lords and ladies. Mid these scholars, statesmen, and philosophers, he blazed "like a
torch amidst the tapers," showing himself
wiser than the scholars, wittier than the
humorists, kinglier than the courtliest. And
yet, in the very prime of his midmanhood,
Burns lay down to die, a broken-hearted
man. He who had sinned much suffered
much, and being the victim of his own
folly, he was also the victim of ingratitude
and misfortune. Bewildered by his debts,
he seems like an untamed eagle beating
against bars he cannot break. The last
time he lifted his pen upon the page it was
not to give immortal form to some exquisite lyric he had fashioned, but to beg a
friend in Edinburgh for a loan of ten pounds
to save him from the terrors of a debtor's
prison. At the summit of his fame,
Walter Scott said that the most precious
treasure his memory possessed was associ-

ated with the moment when as a boy he met Robert Burns and looked into the poet's eyes, dark and tender, "the most glorious eyes" he had ever seen. But the last time that Robert Burns's eyes glowed they blazed with anger against a creditor who had come to drag the dying man from his couch to the prison cell. Possessed by sorrow as with an evil spirit, his dark hair streaked with gray before its time, worn by worries, wasted with fever, imbittered by troubles against which he had bravely struggled, but struggled in vain, like Saul, Burns fell upon an untimely death.

And so this child of sunshine and sweet song, with his flashing wit and abundant laughter, died feeling that his sun was to go down mid clouds as black as have ever been woven out of the warp and woof of poverty and misfortune. Yet he is not one of the prophets whom men have first slain and then builded their sepulcher. Carlyle thinks Burns received more rather than less of the kindnesses usually bestowed upon great teachers. For ours is a world that pays Socrates with a cup of poison, and Christ with a cross. We are told, too, that

Tasso polished his cantos in a madhouse, Cervantes perfected his pages in a prison, Roger Bacon wrought out his principles in a dungeon, Locke was banished and wrote his treatise on the mind while shivering in a Dutch garret, and by contrast with the lot of other worthies Burns seems the child of good fortune. In the last analysis the blame is with the poet himself. Not want of good fortune without, but want of good guidance within, wrecked this youth. Save Saul alone, history holds no sadder tragedy than that of Burns, who sang "the short and simple annals of the poor," songs that have made this singer's name immortal.

But if some explain Burns's excesses and sins by his extreme poverty, urging that penury gave him "no shelter to grow ripe and no leisure to grow wise," in Byron we have one in whom wealth was united to genius, like the costliest vase holding the loveliest flower. Surely, poverty never pinched Byron, and certainly his intellect made the path bright enough for his young feet. Indeed he was the first English author to conquer the admiration of the

Continent. Goethe gave him a place among the foremost. France and Italy bestowed an admiration hitherto reserved for Shakespeare alone. Other gifts also were his. Men called Byron the handsomest youth of his time. His beautiful head, his finely chiseled features, his face glowing with feeling like an alabaster lamp lighted from within, his courtly manners, lent him the note of distinction, and he had the beauty of a Greek god. In language of unrivaled force and beauty, he led the revolt of the common people against the infamous court of George III. Publishing his first volume, he woke one morning to find himself famous.

Yet this youth, so brave, so beautiful, dowered with gifts so rich, perished ere his race was half run. In a reckless, pleasure-loving age, he drank more, lived faster, and was more reckless than any other man. When vice had disturbed his happiness, sin poisoned his genius. Alienated from England, he went to the Continent, and entered upon such escapades as unbridled desires alone suggest. Soon Shelley wrote home that a violent death was the best thing to be desired for Byron. The fever that at last consumed his body was fully matched by the remorse that preyed upon his mind. In his dying hour the worm, the canker, and the grief were his alone. Therefore he likened himself to a serpent, girt about with fire, that turns its poisoned fangs upon itself as a means of escaping from approaching flames. If, in his early career, England would have buried Byron in one of the favorite spots of her abbey, when at length his career ended in disgrace, she closed her great temple against Byron, and his friends bore his troubled dust to the little churchyard at Hucknall. When young Alfred Tennyson heard that Byron was dead, he said, "I thought the world was at an end." Mourning for his fallen hero, Tennyson took up David's lament for Saul: "How are the mighty fallen! Perished are the weapons of the great!"

When we have noted that Poe starved and shivered into the tramp's grave at thirty-nine, that Burns found the wolf at his door at thirty-seven, that the fiend was gnawing at the heartstrings of Byron at thirty-six, that at thirty Shelley passed beyond "the contagion of the world's slow stain," that Keats, "whose name is writ not in water," but in adamant, was dead at twenty-five, we must not interpret these ill-starred lives as meaning that the history of great poets represents defeat and tragedy, while the history of men great in other departments of life represents triumph and victory. If we call the roll of the artists, we find that Andrea del Sarto had gifts so great as to lead many to believe that he was superior to Raphael himself. In his early youth he painted pictures characterized by such beauty and majesty of drawing, such richness of color, as to promise a supremacy altogether unique. But early in his career this youth passed under the influence of a beautiful Jezebel, left his aged parents to starve, and for gold sold his brush to ignoble patrons. When Francis I. advanced money for certain pictures, the youth spent it in riotous living, making no return to his benefactor. Stricken with remorse, he was overtaken by a contagious disease. Deserted by the woman for whom he had abandoned honor, fame, and friends, he perished in the solitude of a filthy garret, and at midnight was hastily carried forth to a pauper's grave.

But in philosophy, also, great men have had a like career. Here is Bacon, with his noble birth, reared in a palace, educated at court, and replying, almost as soon as he could speak, to the queen, asking how old he was, "Two years younger than your Majesty's happy reign." He garnered universal wisdom. He founded a new system of philosophy. He ushered in our era of science and invention. But he also added the cunning of a traitor to the wisdom of a statesman, and the meanness of a slave to the grasp of a philosopher. His soul has been likened to a marble palace—bright in its walls and brave in its battlements, but within foul of cellar and noisome of garret.

Nor are the tragedies less dark in other realms. What a career is that of De Quincey, the essayist. Early in life he fell a slave to the opium habit, that shattered his nerves, darkened his reason, destroyed his happiness and home, and enfeebled his will. He who once had been master to many pupils, leading on like a pillar of fire for brilliancy, became a pillar of cloud, out of which leaped but intermittent flashes—flashes not of light, but of lightning, that served only to deepen the darkness in which the great man dwelt. For De Quincey ended his career, like Samson, blind and grinding corn in the prison of those who once had been his servants.

Pathetic the tragedy of great men in the realm of affairs, also. In his class no man of his time even approached the "Little Corsican" in sheer weight of intellect. He stayed a revolution, conquered kingdoms, made a code, leveled the Alps, invented a system of weights and measures. He was so great that single-handed he might have set France forward a half century in the march of civilization. But prosperity made him proud, power made him cruel, and moving swiftly toward ruin, Emerson says he became unjust to his generals, false to his wife, blind to honor, until he could "steal, lie, slander, drown, and poison, as his interest demanded." Stricken with death upon his lonely island home, he coolly falsified dates, facts, and characters to heighten his fame. For the great general victory became defeat.

Wisdom, also, hath its tragedy. Scholars, from Solomon to Goethe, have gotten wisdom and knowledge, but too often also have indulged themselves in sin, until their making of books seems a vanity, and all their days days of disgrace — whose biographers, like Noah's sons, must needs walk backward to hide the hero's nakedness. And here are the sons of wealth, who have used their superior strength and power to thrust back from life's good things those who are inferior and weak, and who, going toward the throne, have left behind their charming modesty; and becoming proud and imperious, have ruined happiness and made life a tragedy. And here are the daughters of beauty, from Cleopatra to the modern "lily," whose gift was loveliness, whose task it is, to lift men up from the abyss and guide them from star to star, but who have embroiled men in quarrels, brought anarchy into the lives of those who have loved them, whose breath is a pestilence, whose affection is a flame, who have been to men not "the shade of a rock in a weary land," but the sharpness of a rock to sink goodly ships. Oh, the story of greatness is one long, black, piteous tragedy! Happy, thrice happy, those who are the children of one talent or two or three, who dwell neither in the arctic zone of chill penury nor the heated zone of the tropics, but rather in the temperate zone, where the average man doth abide, fulfilling the world's work, above whose bier rises no mournful lament, "How are the mighty fallen!" and "Perished are the weapons of the great!"

Difficult indeed the task of explaining the wreck and ruin of these sons of greatness. In the noblest plea that one man of genius has ever made for another, Carlyle reminds us that the orbit of a planet is large and that of a circus ring small, and that a deflection of a few inches from the small ring would be greater in proportion to its diameter than for the planet to wander thousands of miles from its vast orbit. "Granted," says Carlyle of Burns, "the ship comes into harbor with shroud and tackle damaged; the pilot is blameworthy; he has not been all-wise or all-powerful, but to know how blameworthy tell us first whether his voyage has been round the globe or merely for a yachting trip across some sequestered lake."

But Byron's plea is very bold. He affirms
that greatness sanctifies whatever it does;
that genius is exempt from moral laws that
are binding upon dull people, that his
superior gifts lend the possessor a chartered
right to gratify his desires and passions in
whatsoever garden of pleasure. This plea
would make Burns blameless for clothing
drinking songs with matchless beauty. It
frees Del Sarto from condemnation for hanging immortal wreaths upon the forehead of
Satanic creatures, and discharges the French
school from responsibility for clothing the
worst sentiments in the loveliest language.
But in moments of sober reflection, thoughtful minds will affirm that as men go toward
greatness they go toward responsibility; that
when God gives the youth power and maiden
beauty, He takes vows from them; that fol-
lies quite excusable in a one-talent man are
monstrous in the children of ten talents; that
by virtue of supremacy the children of
strength and genius are pledged to special
honor and purity and justice and truth in the
inner parts. All wise men must hold with
John Milton that greatness is a pledge to
goodness. Explaining his vast intellectual

achievements, Milton said: "He who would write a heroic poem must first live a heroic life. I am not one who has disgraced beauty of sentiment by deformity of conduct, or the maxims of the free man by the actions of the slave, but by the grace of God I have kept my life unsullied. I take God to witness that in all those places where so many things are considered lawful I have lived sound and untouched from any profligacy and vice, having this thought perpetually with me, that though I might escape the eyes of men, I certainly could not escape the eyes of God."

Having confessed the overthrow of the sons of greatness, Robert Browning meditates the soul's recovery also. The majesty of its thoughts, the splendor of its imagery, the simplicity and sweetness of its rhythmic flow make his "Saul" one of the greatest of Browning's poems. In that hour when sin had bewildered the king's intellect and melancholy enfeebled his will, growing desperate, Saul denied himself food and drink and withdrew into his innermost tent. When three days and nights had come and gone, with no sign of life from the royal sufferer, his servants in frightened whispers talked much upon death. They dared not cross the forbidden threshold. Soon his faithful general grew desperate. Having watched the long night through, when morning came he bethought himself that perhaps young David might seek entrance in the sacred name of friendship. For all too much this king had lived alone. A little solitude nurtures strength, but continued solitude threatens the very center of man's being. Of necessity the mountain peak that rises above its fellows must dwell apart, and it is the peril of the great that at last they are alone, none daring to expose the strong man's peril or lay bare his secret faults. Yet for a thousand reasons the great have special need of sympathy and friendship. Hours there are when the world reels beneath man's feet, when trouble chokes his voice, and then each Saul must lean upon some bosom friend. For ours is a world where the fireman climbing the ladder to certain death is strengthened by the cheers of onlookers.

Entering the battle, the young soldier is

less afraid because of his brave companions. Oft in moments when sorrow breaks
the heart one look into the face of a friend
whose eyes are dim with tears is worth all
gifts of gold. Cicero says, "Friendship can
make riches splendid." But Friendship
worketh other miracles. When winter's frost
makes great cracks in the asphalt street,
workmen force a tongue of flame upon the
injured parts, and soon the warm glow
unites parts that before were separated.
And it is given to love's warm flame to
repair the grievous injuries that sin hath
wrought in the soul. In the olden time,
when the sufferer touched the hem of
Christ's garment, electric life leaped from
Saviour to sufferer. Then one touch of the
hand, a glance, a kindly deed, the sympathetic note—medicines these that heal the
broken heart. Browning would have us
believe that the recovery of every Saul begins with these words, "In my darkest
hour there came a friend."

Standing at the door, beyond which lay
the broken-hearted king, David pondered
what form of message he should bring.
Times there are when silence is a medicine.

In other hours speech hath its ministry. If David feared not his battle with Goliath, he trembled exceedingly as he began his struggle to recover Saul's soul. Taking his harp in his hand, he breathed a prayer that God would teach him the ministry of sweet song. If the other arts can inspire and instruct, music can redeem and save. As the fine arts go away from God's throne they lose their flexibility and take on forms hard and permanent. Architecture is the lowest of the fine arts; it is most permanent. Sculpture is higher, but the statue is cold, having form alone. To form painting adds color, and breathes warm tints of life. Literature is a higher art, using words for colors. But music is builded of breath alone and dies with the vibrating air. The least permanent art, it is also the highest. If worship begins with the foundations of the cathedral, it ends with the song that is a golden chariot upon which the soul rides forth to meet its God. On that Christmas night the shepherds said that Christ was born to sound of angelic music. And if the soul enters the earthly scene mid melodious notes, the dying man also asks to pass away while some sweet song wafts him home to heaven. Richter says "music restores childhood." In the hour, therefore, when Saul was drear and stark, dumb and deaf, David tuned his harp, took off the lilies that twined its chords, and sang of love and home and heaven, sang of God's mercy that forgives and saves.

Impressive indeed, that scene when David stood before the fallen king, plying him by light and darkness, by hope and fear, by the memories of the past, by the hopes of the future, rebuking Saul, fighting him, controlling, and at last conquering him by truths divine. Recalling the days when Saul's heart was young, David sang the song with which the shepherd calls his flock, and carried the darkened king back to well-remembered scenes. He sang the harvest song, and brought back the days when the youth had led the reapers into the fields of golden grain. He rehearsed the events of war, the coming of an invading host, the tramp of armed men, the hours when Saul, the leader, buckled on his armor, the fierce shock of the battle, and the moment of final victory. Justifying the

ways of God to man, he reminded Saul that
trouble hath its ministry and suffering its
mercy; that the stroke of the lightning, not
less than the falling dew, nurtures the
sheaves of harvest; that the sweetest per-
fume comes from bruised flowers; that if
the palm tree dies, its dates will live to support men crossing life's desert, and if old
age is a winter that strips the trees of
leaves, the leaves fall only to lend a lovelier
luster to the boughs of May. Therefore,
good deeds done, truth sown as seeds, shall
rise again in new harvests of beauty. And
having plied Saul by the memories of childhood and youth, by his ambitions and
victories, his temptations and sufferings, his
prayers and tears, suddenly David swings
wide for him the door of immortality, and
reminds this man, with his sorrow and
shame and failure, that through God's good
mercy the immortal life shall repair the
defeats of the life that is. An eternal morn
shall succeed death's brief night. Saul,
now a ruin and a failure, shall awake to
new light and new life and endure.

By the pain throb triumphantly winning intensified
bliss
And the next world's reward and repose by struggles
in this.

And then, because David believes that the

> Acknowledgment of God in Christ,
> Accepted by the reason, solves for thee
> All questions in the world and out of it,

he points this baffled, wounded, fainting
king to that mysterious double star shining
forth in man's dark night. "Would I suffer
for him I love?" exclaims Browning.
"Then so will God, so will God."

O Saul, it shall be
A face like my face that receives thee, a man like to
me
Thou shalt love and be loved by forever!
  A hand like this hand
Shall throw open the gates of new life to thee,
  See the Christ stand!

Behold the Friend Divine, who is abroad,
recovering men from ruin and defeat.
Therefore hope thou in Christ! His love
can soften the hardest heart, forgive the
blackest sin, can redeem the darkest tragedy
unto triumph and victory.

VIII

The Memoirs of Henry Drummond, and
the Dawn of an Era of Friendship between Science and Religion

In his brief life we saw him pass through two of the greatest trials to which character can be exposed. We watched him, our fellow-student and not yet twenty-three, surprised by a sudden and a fierce fame. Crowds of men and women in all the great cities of our land hung upon his lips, innumerable lives opened their secrets to him, and made him aware of his power over them. When his first book was published, he, being then about thirty-three, found another world at his feet; the great of the land thronged him; his social opportunities were boundless; and he was urged by the chief statesman of our time to a political career. This is the kind of trial which one has seen wither some of the finest characters, and distract others from the simplicity and resolution of their youth. He passed through it unscathed; it neither warped his spirit nor turned him from his accepted vocation as a teacher of religion.

Again, in the end of his life, he was plunged to the opposite extreme. For two long years he not only suffered weakness and excruciating pain, but what must have been more trying to a spirit like his, accustomed all his manhood to be giving, helping, and leading, he became absolutely dependent upon others. This also he bore unspoiled, and we who had known him from the beginning found him at the end the same humble, unselfish, and cheerful friend whom we loved when we sat together on the benches at college.
—*The Life of Henry Drummond, pp. 1, 2.*

Great Books as Life-Teachers

VIII

THE MEMOIRS OF HENRY DRUMMOND, AND THE DAWN OF AN ERA OF FRIENDSHIP BETWEEN SCIENCE AND RELIGION

Our age has been sadly injured by the warfare between theology and science. For some cause, reason and faith have assumed the attitude of enemies, turning the world into a battlefield, and making life one long tournament. Fierce and bitter has been the strife. Often the very skies have seemed to rain pamphlets of attack and defense. A thousand times the skeptics have announced the Waterloo of Christianity and preached the funeral sermon of the Bible, and a thousand times not Christianity, but its enemy, has gone the way to the graveyard. When the scholar reads those volumes of President White called "The History of the Warfare of Science and Theology," he is conscious of the conviction that if theologians have been strangely ignorant of the laws of biology, chemistry, and physics, scientists have been equally ignorant of the laws of self-consciousness, intuition, and spiritual vision. Carlyle and Maurice were seers, and Huxley and Tyndall were scientists, but when a scientist fronts a seer, straightway the sword flies from its scabbard and conversation becomes a tournament.

When some Darwin drops Carlyle's "Sartor Resartus," he exclaims, "It is all mist!" When some Carlyle lays aside Darwin's volume, he exclaims, "It is all mud!" "You theists cannot think!" asserts some Spencer. "You scientists cannot aspire or pray!" returns some Martineau. Professor Huxley had a "fine frenzy" for facts, and in *The Fortnightly Review* made a study of what he called "The Bedevilment of the Gadarene Swine," asserting that the Bible includes many errors of science and history, and falls with these errors, to which his opponent made answer that hundreds of years after Moses made his mistake as to the sun moving around the earth scientists were still teaching that the world rested on an elephant's back, the elephant on four turtles, the turtles on mid-air, and that the history of the blunders of scientists through the centuries would be a volume ten times as thick as the history of the exploded theories in the realm of ethics and morals. When President White ended his volume on the centuries of warfare between scientists and theologians, he might have told us a wonder tale—how two enemies of the olden time were wondrous strange, in that one wore a hat so large as to hide the sky, while the seven-leagued boots of the other were so big that he could not see the earth. Neither science nor theology is infallible. Perhaps the mistakes of the one have been fully equalled by the mistakes of the other. Limited to the realm of the senses, science has its frontier lines. But the queen of the sciences also has her limitations—severe and exacting. Meanwhile, through all the tumult and din of the fierce discussion,

"The little birds sang east, the little birds sang west,
And I smiled to think God's greatness
Flowed around our incompleteness,
Round our restlessness—His rest."

Among the prophets of the new era of
friendship between science and religion let
us include the name of Professor Drummond.
This scientist loved his scalpel and micro-
scope, but he also loved his mother's Bible.
Loving to observe and analyze, he also
loved to hope and pray. Being at once scientist and Christian, he believed that law
was love and love was law. "Whom God
hath crowned, man may not discrown,"
and now that he hath passed beyond the
veil we all do see that Professor Drummond was a prophet of reconciliation and
hath a place among our great leaders. Tirelessly did the reverent scholar study his
Darwin, Wallace, and Spencer, and all those
specialists who have scrutinized the world
of matter. But he also loved his Plato
and Paul and Kant, and with them explored
the realms of mind. He believed indeed
in clods and paving-stones. He also knew
that a thought is just as real a thing as a
cannon ball; that an aspiration is a force as
truly as is the bullet. He knew that the
clod could grow the violet or anemone, and
he also knew that a thought could nourish
generous deeds and heroic purposes that will

endure when clods have dissolved and paving-stones become dust.

Not four years have passed by since Professor Drummond visited the colleges of this New World. Those whose good fortune it was to hear Mr. Drummond will recall the patrician face and form, the finely cut features, the countenance suffused with solar light, the great, rich, wonderful soul throbbing and blushing behind its defenses of flesh and cuticle. He seemed what the lower class men in his university called him, *the Prince*. In his addresses to college students the author of "Natural Law in the Spiritual World" stood forth the reconciler of science and faith.

The laws of light and heat and gravity upon one side of a river are identical with those laws upon the farther shore. In his argument Mr. Drummond asserted that the soul in its critical hours is controlled by the laws of God as truly as suns and planets that sweep forward under the embrace of physical laws. While this seer and scientist spake, how easy to be a scientist in the realm that is seen! How easy, also, to be a Christian, toward the realm

that is unseen! At the noblest vantage
point in Paris stands the Arch de Triomphe,
a central point to which all streets converge.
And while this gifted man reasoned of the
world of matter and the world of mind, men
felt that all the paths of faith and science
converge toward Jesus Christ. If the physi-
cists moved along the pathway of matter,
Drummond was found walking in the way
with them. If the Christian moved along
the pathway of faith, lo! Drummond was
found walking in the way with him! Recalling that hour, scientist and Christian alike
might well say, "Did not our hearts burn
within us, as he opened unto us the way,
the words, and the works of God?"

If we are to rightly estimate Professor
Drummond's contribution to modern knowledge, we must go back in thought to the
conditions that prevailed a generation ago.
In 1850, when Emerson and Carlyle, Darwin and Tyndall, were young men, the new
doctrine of evolution began to make wide
and deep the chasm between science and
theology, so that the seer felt he could not
pass over to the scientist, while the scientist
thought he could not cross over to the seer.

In those days many religious teachers held
that the Bible was a book of geology, astronomy, and politics, as well as a book of
morals; that as yet scarcely six thousand
summers had passed over our earth; that
the story of Jonah and the story of Adam
and Eve were sober history rather than
inspiring parable, and so far from the Bible
being a book of progressive revelation, that
it was, verbally and literally, the book of
God.

Over against this group of noble Puritans,
who have achieved great things for law and
liberty and free institutions, stood the
group of men whose Bible was the book of
nature. With a great, deep love for things
seen, they studied rocks with the lichens
upon them, seeds and the shrubs that
sprang therefrom, while buds, birds, and
beasts were analyzed and compared. Darwin
went down into the sea to study its ooze;
Tyndall climbed the Matterhorn to study
the forms of water in snowflakes and ice
crystal; Lyall and Miller read the writings
of the rock pages; Spencer noted how bark
huts became marble houses; how the fig leaf
became a woolen garment; how the rude

pictures upon the Indian's blanket became
at last the canvas of a great artist; how the
king, who was a Hercules in body, gave
place to Gladstone, the Hercules in mind;
how the clay idol and the drum of the
magician gave place to the great cathedral
and the noble litany.

In the first flush of enthusiasm for the
new generalization, everything was claimed
for the formula of evolution. The early
vagaries of those who were intoxicated with
the great discovery now seem almost incred-
ible. Like the German who had never seen
a picture of an elephant, and therefore
evolved one out of his inner consciousness,
so Professor Huxley evolved his bathybius.
This bathybius was said to be a vast sheet
of gelatin matter lying under the ocean (just
as "the mother" exists in the vinegar),
being, indeed, the mother of all things that
live in land or sea or sky. Unfortunately
the scientists with their dredging machines
soon discovered that "the bathybius" had
no real existence, and was as mythical as the
wooden horse of Homer. Other statements
equally extreme tended to further the prejudice against materialistic evolution, notably

the assertion that the steam engine, a cylin-
der press, and an "Iliad" or a "Hamlet"
are all latent in the fire-mist and the rain-
cloud.

Midway between the theologians holding
the old views and the scientists holding the
new views stood a great body of citizens,
thoughtful and scholarly, who soon pro-
nounced the old theology and the new science alike untenable. Men of reflection
felt that, in view of the discoveries of
geology, it was asking too much of reason
to believe that the earth was made in six
days, or to hold to the cosmogony of Gen-
esis. But these citizens also felt that science
taxed their credulity too far in making the
clod to be the creator of a violet, or a drop
of ooze from the swamp write the "Odyssey"
or "Iliad." Children reading "The Arabian Nights" may believe that a magician
can call a flower, a monkey, and a man
from his magic jug. But wise men decline
to believe that force, even when spelled with
a capital F, can plan the wing of a bird, the
hues of a violet, the beauty of a babe, the
poem or oration of sage or seer. A lump
of mud does not become a creator when

spelled with a capital M, and God cannot be expelled from His universe by being spelled with a small g.

When a few years had passed by, men who were neither theologians nor scientists, like Tennyson and Browning, Ruskin and Carlyle and Emerson, began to make themselves heard. "If man," said Browning, "is buffeted about by fate and chance, if he comes from the earth and goes to the earth, then time is a maniac, scattering dust and life a fury slinging flame." Tennyson asserted that "if man is to be blown about the desert dust or sealed within the iron hills, then he is a monster, a dream, a discord, and dragons of the prime that tear each other in their slime are mellow music matched with him." When Matthew Arnold discerned that morality seemed likely to fall with the fall of the religious sentiment, he straightway began to ascribe to the unknown one after another of the divine attributes.

The traveler on Mount Rigi receives from his guide a bit of rose-colored glass through which the clouds glow and flame. But should the weary traveler stretch out his hand and break off a chunk of damp cloud, the fact that the cloud was suffused with light would make it a poor substitute for the wheaten loaf. Considered as a color effect, "the suffusing of morality, with emotion" is highly successful; considered as a substitute for God, it seems somewhat insufficient. Romanes, one of the most gifted of all the disciples of Darwin, returned to his Christian faith, and asserted that he knew no formula of evolution that did not require an infinite God to make it workable. Evolution began to be theistic. Scientists used it to describe God's way of doing things. Men like Clerk Maxwell, Professor Balfour, Professor Tait, Sir William Thomson, St. George Mivart, and Romanes began to declare that science and theology alike were both right and wrong. As time went on it was discovered that the young men in the colleges and universities, under the head of President McCosh and Professor Le Conte and John Fiske, were emphasizing the words "Christian evolution." Lord Salisbury, the present premier of England, in his annual address as president of the Association for the Advancement of Science, affirmed that the tendency of the latest science was unequivocally and aggressively toward theism, indeed, but also toward a simple Christian faith.

How great is the change that has passed over the world of scientific thought may be inferred from an authorized statement by a well-known fellow of the Royal Society of London: "I have known the British association under forty-one different presidents, all leading men of science, with the exception of two or three appointed on other grounds. On looking over these forty-one names I counted twenty-one who are men of Christian belief and character, while only four disbelieved in any divine revelation. These figures indicate that religious faith, rather than unbelief, has characterized the leading men of the association."

At the moment when the thoughts of men were busiest on the relation of religion and science, Professor Drummond published his first book, called "Natural Law in the Spiritual World." The essence of this epoch-making volume is that evolution is the supreme word for religion, as well as for science. But by evolution Mr. Drummond did not mean Darwinism, for that is a proposition as yet unproved; nor Spencerianism, which is as yet incomplete; nor Weismanism, which is in the hottest fires of criticism; but evolution as a generic term, setting forth God's way of doing things; for this young knight of the new era believed in God with all his heart and mind and soul and strength.

When that statue, Venus de Milo, was unearthed by a peasant plowing in the field, men explained its beauty by assuming a sculptor whose genius was fully equal to such beauty wrought into the marble. And behind the dim unknown, beneath the mountains, in the deep depths beyond Orion and the Pleiades, Drummond saw the garments of an unseen God, the God of unity and law and love. He beheld the Creator pour form and beauty into all things that are. He saw an incandescent, nebulous mass, flinging off its outer rings, those rings cooling into planetary systems; this red-hot earth put on an outer crust; the ice-plow crush rocks into dust for soil; in a vision hour he beheld the source of all life breathe life into matter dead hitherto; he heard the Divine Voice command the soil to ascend toward shrub and tree; animals also joined the strange upward procession; afar off he beheld the face of our father man; he saw man a rude, low savage, schooled by heat and cold and hunger, and while he beheld the savage, he threw away his war club or fashioned it into a plow handle. Imitating the bee hiving its sweets, a granary was founded and filled. Inspired from above, he saw the tepees give place to cities, where arts, industries, laws, liberty, religion, reigned. In an hour of beatific vision he saw earth exhaling spirits into the open heavens, where life went on and men went upward, increasing in knowledge and happiness and love. Remembering that Christ said, "First the blade, then the ear, then the full corn in the ear," Drummond asserted that evolution was the one supreme word for religion, the greatest generalization our world has ever known.

Professor Drummond was scarcely five and thirty years of age when he placed the manuscript of "Natural Law in the Spiritual World" in the hands of his printer and started to the Dark Continent, to write his book on "Tropical Africa." When the sci-

entist returned he found himself famous.
His book was the most striking success of
the year; his fascinating theories were being
discussed in every great journal and review;
his name had become a household word in
two continents. Seldom, if ever, has a
philosophical work created so great a sensation. Now that ten years have passed by,
we know that his pages have a permanent
fascination. The gist of the volume is the
analogy between God's laws in the realm of
matter and His laws in the realm of spirit.
The scholar noted that Huxley and Tyndall
denied the possibility of spontaneous life.
These scientists used heat to kill the germs
of life in water, and then sealed the water up
in jars. When long time had passed, they
found the water as devoid of life as is a
piece of ice. They asserted that, though
millions of years passed, a piece of rock and
a drop of water were absolutely devoid of
power to generate life. "Science knows,"
said Professor Huxley, "that life comes
only from life."

Having noted that once a plant is alive
it can throw down its roots to crystals
and gases and clothe them with the mys-

tery of life, Drummond also affirmed that spiritual life is not spontaneous, but is breathed by God into the soul of each publican, or each Saul on his way to Damascus, and that once touched with this breath of life and love, man could clothe his every thought and deed with the mystery of this new spiritual impulse. Having justified the great crisis of the soul called repentance and conversion, as exhibited in some Luther or Paul, Drummond goes on to study the problem of degeneration and death. A rock is dead because it has no relation with the world outside; a plant has a little life because it has its root; a bird is related to the air as well as to earth; man adds many vital functions. If life is an increase of correspondence, death is the cutting of the nerves of relation. Cut off the nerve of sight, and color dies; cut the nerve of hearing, and sound dies; cut the nerve of sensation, and movement dies; cut the nerve of food, and the last tie is sundered, and death is complete. How fascinating Drummond's study of the problem of culture, growth, parasitism, classification, eternal life! "If the Bible shows how to go to heaven," nature, interpreted by Drummond, shows "how the heaven goeth."

Mr. Drummond's last book is upon "The Ascent of Man." This is a study of the human body, fearfully and wonderfully made, through the long processes of nature and God. Drummond viewed the body as an intricate and complicated sensorium, a delicate and complex mechanism, with eye and ear and outer sense, as open windows through which rushed the world of truth and beauty, color, sound, and sense. Guided by the embryologists, the scientist notes that each individual man passes through the stages of fish, bird, and mammal, and is at last born an embryonic man. In the body of the babe are compacted all achievements of the entire animal world, each bone, each nerve, each ganglion. It is as if "the modern stem-winding watch should assemble all the features of the old time-keepers every minute." It is as if the modern loom should assemble all the features of all the looms since the time of Arkwright. It is as if the modern locomotive should include every cog and wheel used by all inventors since the time of Watt. In reality the last loco-

motive includes only the best features of
former engines. Strangely enough, the
human embryo includes every phase of life
known to every animal creature, as if man
had passed through the experience of all.
Astronomers discovered the planet Nep-
tune after its existence had been predicted
from the disturbance induced in the orbit of
Uranus. Drummond noted that, while the
adult man has only twelve pairs of ribs and
certain animals have fourteen, it was predicted that in a certain stage the infantile
man would be found with fourteen pairs, a
prediction that was actually verified. Studying the scaffolding of the body, the scientist
mentions some fifty or sixty organs—e. g.,
vermiform appendix—that are vestiges of
powers once highly useful, but now being
slowly atrophied. The lower animals ascend
the witness stand and testify as to the origin
of man's body. He notes the arrest of
the body, and affirms that the earth will
never know a higher creature than man.
His argument is very plain. The time was
when man developed his hands through
use, but now the loom and the lathe toil for
his hands. The time was when man's legs

had many duties; now their contracts are fulfilled by steam and electricity, and the development of the limbs has been arrested. Once the eye and the ear were very acute, but now the lenses of the optician have arrested the development of the eye.

In those fascinating chapters called "The Evolution of the Father and Mother" Mr. Drummond shows how the law of force and the survival of the fittest became the law of love and self-sacrifice. In times past the strongest alone survived, while the weak went to the wall. But motherhood came to lift the shield above weakness. Love caused weakness to survive. In motherhood egotism became altruism and force was transmuted into self-sacrifice. Slowly God taught the strong to bear the burdens of the weak. Father and mother, through personal experience, came to understand God as the world's larger Father and great burden bearer. At last to man was revealed God as washing the feet of each insect, caring for each lily and sparrow, bearing man's ignorance and weakness and sin. In the fullness of time God had lifted man so high that at last, before man's wondering vision, there was unveiled the face of that one who "seemest human and divine," Jesus Christ, the world's supreme guide and teacher, the ideal of all that is best for man, the revelation of all that is truest and sweetest in the God of infinite love.

If Martin Luther and Bishop Butler came at a strategic hour, it was the good fortune of Professor Drummond to speak at one of those psychological moments when the world, eager and expectant, waited for some prophet of reconciliation. Not an intellectual giant himself, it was given him to usher in an era of friendship between giants hitherto at enmity. He taught the world that it was possible to be a rigid scientist and also a sweet-hearted Christian. With him character was a thousand times more than culture, and Christ's words about the soul were infinitely more important than man's words about sticks, stones, and stars. The title of one of his books, "Love, the Greatest Thing in the World," contains the genius of his practical teachings. He used to say that if man cared for quantity, God cared for quality. In his philosophy one Christ-cultured life is worth more to a nation and a city than a hundred thousand ordinary persons. In wounded vanity, disappointed hopes, and selfish chagrin he found the "vulgar universal sources of man's unrest." But as no fever can attack a perfectly sound body, so Professor Drummond thought "no fever of unrest can disturb a soul which breathes the air or learns the ways of Christ." Stricken with death, this Christian scientist said: "Men sigh for the wings of a dove that they may fly away and be at rest. But flying away will not help them. The kingdom of God is within you. It is Christ that teaches the secret of the great calm and the invulnerable faith." Then with untroubled heart the seer and scientist fell asleep, and

"Passed to where, beyond these voices, there is rest and peace."

IX

The Opportunities of Leisure and Wealth, an Outlook upon the Life of Lord Shaftesbury

And Sir Launfal said, "I behold in thee
An image of Him who died on the tree;"

He parted in twain his single crust,
He broke the ice on the streamlet's brink,
And gave the leper to eat and drink,
'Twas a mouldy crust of coarse brown bread,
'Twas water out of a wooden bowl,—
Yet with fine wheaten bread was the leper fed,
And 'twas red wine he drank with his thirsty soul.

As Sir Launfal mused with downcast face,
A light shone round about the place;
The leper no longer crouched at his side,
But stood before him glorified,
Shining and tall and fair and straight
 As the pillar that stood by the Beautiful Gate,—
Himself the Gate whereby men can
Enter the temple of God in Man.

"Lo, it is I, be not afraid!
In many climes, without avail,
Thou hast spent thy life for the Holy Grail;
Behold, it is here,—this cup which thou
Didst fill at the streamlet for me but now;
This crust is my body broken for thee,
This water his blood that died on the tree;
The Holy Supper is kept, indeed,
In whatso we share with another's need;
Not what we give, but what we share,
For the gift without the giver is bare;
Who gives himself with his alms feeds three,
Himself, his hungering neighbor, and me."

The Vision of Sir Launfal (*Lowell*), *pp. 301, 302, 303.*

IX

THE OPPORTUNITIES OF LEISURE AND WEALTH, AN OUTLOOK UPON THE LIFE OF LORD SHAFTESBURY

In all ages the human heart has hungered for heroes. Every generation has sought some forehead over which to break its alabaster box, some feet at which to empty out all its flowers, its love, its tears. The quality of hero the age has admired gives the measure of the nation's civilization. Long centuries ago Cicero ranked his city low in the scale of progress, because there were few citizens who loved eloquence or philosophy or art, but many who crowded after the golden chariot of the conqueror. In Tasso's time the sentiment had changed, for one day when Michael Angelo completed the lustrous angels on the ceiling of the Sistine chapel the admiring multitude tore his brushes into fragments for mementos, and making a chariot of their arms, bore the artist home to his lodgings.

A little later, in Scotland, the ideal hero was a patriot. It was Robert Bruce who cast the sacred spell upon the people. He who wished to be enshrined in human hearts must die upon the battlefield and with his blood make beautiful some flag of liberty. It is the glory of our age that the modern hero stands forth armed not with swords and spears, but weaponed with love and kindness, with service and sympathy. The new knight errant toils for the orphan and the invalid, or labors for the children of the unhappy poor. It was the misfortune of the ancient era that it taught Ulysses how to bend his bow, but not what to shoot; taught Ajax how to forge iron, but left him to fashion the metal into manacles for slaves; taught Gutenberg how to use movable type, but not what ideas to print; taught Galileo's age how to use the telescope and see the stars distant millions of miles, but not how to see the woes and wrongs in the next street, the sorrows of serfs and slaves, the distress of debtors and prisoners.

"The peril of the republic," said Carlyle, "will be the misgovernment of its great cities." Now that fifty years have passed the prophecy has become history, and our large towns have passed under the rule of Circe's cup. The great scholar saw that in a world where leisure alone makes men masters in the realm of learning, leisure must also be invoked to make men masters in the art of governing great cities. But if Carlyle discerned that the dominion of the demagogue could be broken by the rule of a leisure class, in our time a thousand new considerations emphasize his thought. To-day an enemy is abroad in the land, sowing tares by day and by night, lighting the flames of class hatred.

Strangely enough the objects of hatred are those who in times past have been deemed most serviceable to the community. In the city he who by saving what other men wasted has produced $500,000 is a plutocrat and a baron; in the town he who has $50,000 is the public enemy; in the remote community he who has $10,000 is the object of scorn and attack; while in Kentucky recently, when a group of tramps, making their usual winter excursion into the South, met a young traveling peddler, they were so incensed against this plutocrat who had one handbag and two bundles of knickknacks, where they had only rags, that they fell upon this youth, and finding in his knapsack indubitable proofs of wickedness, they beat him as an enemy of the human race and left him half dead.

If the republic is to go forward unto better laws, happier homes, greater happiness, to the toil of the working classes must be added the toil of the leisure classes. Our jails are full, our haunts of vice are full, our reputation as hoodlums is also fully established. But in the light of what Ruskin and Shaftesbury accomplished for London, should a score of men and women of the leisure class give their lives to the higher life of this community, an affirmative answer might be given to that momentous question, "Can we make ours a true city of God?"

To every department of nature and life God has given its own voice and prophet. Each stone and star, each bird and beast, hath its special advocate. To the planets God gave Newton, to the bees Huber, Linnæus to the plants, Audubon to the birds, Phillips to the slave, Nightingale to the soldiers, Livingstone to the savage. Having given Ruskin as a voice to genius, He gave Shaftesbury as a voice for social position and rank. "The history of the progress of the working classes in this century," said the present prime minister of England, "is very largely the history of one man's life—that of Shaftesbury." Very early in his career this child of high rank and wealth received from God a retainer against every form of oppression and wrong. Of his unique talents it has been said that greatness was hereditary in that distinguished family.

Like the famous vine in Hampton Court, with its proportions of a forest tree, his ancestral stalk had for generations ripened great mental treasure. But to the gifts of high birth were added the enrichment of Harrow and Oxford; afterward came several years of travel, expelling narrowness and prejudice, and making the youth a citizen of the universe. This child of good fortune was only five-and-twenty when he took his place in Parliament, yet as the young lark strikes a few notes of sweet song when only a few weeks have passed over its life, so very early in his career this youth made a revelation of his innermost spirit and genius. One winter's night he was sitting with a member of the cabinet beside his fireplace watching the flames and the sparks fly up the chimney. Within all was beauty, comfort, and happiness, but without the sleet and wind were beating upon the window, and in the winter's blast and darkness wandered full many an orphan boy. At ten o'clock the young man excused himself to his host and started out to look for some unfortunate, lost in the darkness and cold, even as the monks and their faithful dogs of the St. Bernard monastery go forth in the storm to save travelers lost in the snow. At that time Shaftesbury had hired a shelter house in the east end of London, near Whitechapel road.

Very pathetic was that midnight scene. With his lantern and his two hired helpers Shaftesbury made his way to the end of London bridge, where he knew he would find twenty or thirty men huddled up close together to keep warm. As his lantern fell upon their faces, one and another, pricked by conscience, would leap to his feet and spring quickly into the darkness. Soon he learned where were the sheltered spots in which the unfortunates hid themselves, the ends of bridges where newsboys nestled, the stairways that offered shelter to wanderers, the homes of vice, the haunts of crime. Before two o'clock the next morning Shaftesbury had collected some thirty boys and men and led them away to his new shelter, where each received his bowl of soup and loaf of bread, his bath, and thick blanket for the night's rest. For more than forty years, when parliament rose at midnight and other members went home, it was Shaftesbury's custom to go forth to search out those of whom Christ said, "I was sick and in prison and ye visited me." "Inasmuch as ye have done it unto one of the least of these my brethren, ye have done it unto me."

The artist who would paint this man, who was one of the most distinguished members of Parliament, and also of her Majesty's government, must represent the tall figure, refined face, and the patrician posture, not as he stood upright, delivering some speech in the house, but rather as he stooped to flash his lantern upon the wanderers sleeping at midnight under

Waterloo bridge. But let no man underestimate Shaftesbury's self-denial. The traveler who has visited the ancestral home, driven through the long avenue of beeches and elms, entered the mansion with its towers and turrets, looked into the faces of those six earls who went before Shaftesbury, or stood in the vast library or galleries with their treasures, alone can understand what Shaftesbury denied himself when he turned from his elegant opulence and refined leisure to spend his nights and days in alleviating the woes of the poor. He loved music and the drama, and did much to advance their interests. He loved the company of scholars and statesmen; he loved great men and gracious women. But he held his rank and position as trusts in the interest of weakness. Whoever came to him in trouble brought a message from God —his trouble being a letter of introduction. Homer tells us that when a celestial being visited the battlefield of Troy and saw the gash in the foot of Patrocles she shed bitter tears and turned away from the grewsome sight. Shaftesbury also could not pass misfortune without shedding tears, yet he fled not away from want, but rather to want, that he might stanch the wound and heal the woe.

The first of Shaftesbury's great reform movements was in the interests of that class of London's poor termed the street arabs, the waifs and strays of the metropolis. These were the children of the most ignorant class, as sturdy of growth as weeds in a wheatfield. They swarmed the streets, they gamboled in the gutters, they haunted the markets in search of castaway food, they nested under porches and stairways, they crept into stables or under arches for lodgings. They lived as the dogs of Constantinople live, the outcasts of the great city. The statesman saw that such an atmosphere could no more rear good citizens than the breath of hot Vesuvius could cover the mountains with roses and violets. One Sunday afternoon in 1840 Shaftesbury took the celebrated Arnold of Rugby for a tour through Bloomsbury, noted for its filth and fever, its haunts of vice and crime.

The memory of that visit haunted Arnold by day and night for weeks afterward. "These classes," he wrote, "form the riddle of our civilization, and may yet destroy us as did the Vandals of old." In order to acquaint himself fully with the problems of the poor, for ten years Shaftesbury gave his Sunday afternoons, and often the mornings of his week days, to the exploration of the lanes and alleys of the tenement house districts. In his report to Parliament he speaks of houses so foul that his physician had to stand outside the door to write the prescription; of walls that oozed grime; of rookeries whose bricks sweat filth; of a cellar where four families occupied the single room, with chalk lines marking the boundaries of each. After conducting the committee appointed by Parliament through this region, he reported that one-fourth of the inhabitants of the great metropolis were born amid these filthy surroundings. He reminded England that the schoolhouse must go before the ballot-box, and that if each outcast child was some day to use his vote and rule like a king, the threshold of the schoolroom must be made as attractive for the boys as the threshold of a king's palace.

The romantic story of how Shaftesbury founded fifty or more "ragged" schools, attended by some ten thousand children, is now a part of history, as is his system of night schools, industrial schools, and Sunday schools, where boys and girls were taught not only sacred truths, but also how to make their own clothes, how to weave doormats, make hassocks, print handbills, mastering many of the simpler handicrafts. The thrilling story of how Shaftesbury covered all London with his schoolrooms, that with their transformations wrought upon child life—because sacred as sanctuaries—comes to us with the force of divine indictment, for in the great cities of our land, awaiting the friendship of the leisure classes, are many hundreds of thousands of children whose footsteps never cross the threshold of a Bible school, who have never had childhood softened by its music, nor manhood molded by its lesson.

Shaftesbury's movements in the interest of the working girls and shopwomen of London throws a flood of light upon one of the most vexed questions of our own city. In New York wise men have successfully inaugurated a system of small loans for the poor, through pawnshops that are largely the outcome of Shaftesbury's first enterprise. Having founded several homes for poor girls and working women, he found that many who sold flowers and water-cress during the summer were without employment during the four months of winter, when most of all they needed it, nor had they the money to prepare to enter a new occupation adapted to the cold season. Lord Shaftesbury therefore conceived the idea of founding a loan association to assist women to support their families.

His agents bought chocolate and coffee stalls, waffle boards and "baked potato ovens," while for boys, money was loaned to buy the outfit for boot blacking. During one winter he made loans of from one to two pounds each among a thousand poor women, whose daily toil was the sole support of an entire family. In reviewing his loans for twenty years he found that during the period his entire losses were less than fifty pounds, and these were through sickness or death of the borrower rather than through fraud. In no case was it necessary to enforce the payment by taking away the ovens or stands. Most of this money was repaid at the rate of a sixpence or a shilling per week. Referring to one poor creature whom he had picked up at night, he says: "One night I found a stranded bit of driftwood. She seemed heartbroken, and I started her in business with a cress and coffee stand. Her fidelity and service of love among the poor in the years since her reform have made her a veritable angel of mercy in the tenement district where she lives. During a long life I have proved that not one kind word ever spoken, not one kind deed ever done, but sooner or later returns to bless the giver, and becomes a chain binding men with golden bands to the throne of God."

Extending his reforms into other realms, Shaftesbury began to look into the lodging-house system. First he erected in the tenement house district a home for young men just in from the country who wanted to find a place where the decencies of life were observed, and wished shelter for a moderate rent. He saw to it that each room was well lighted, ventilated, and had the best sanitary provisions, adding some conveniences then called luxuries. To his great astonishment the enterprise that was begun as a benefaction ended as an investment paying six per cent. But all about were thousands of old tenements falling into decay and breeding physical pestilence and moral death. With tireless enthusiasm he set about purging this reeking inferno, a task that involved ten of the best years of his life.

Interesting Peabody, the Boston banker, Shaftesbury prepared a bill that provided for the condemnation and destruction of hundreds of old houses, while in the specifications for new buildings regard was had for sunshine, air, and the size of the rooms, their periodic whitewashing and cleansing, and the number of persons who could occupy a given house. This was the first successful effort to reach the very dregs of poverty, and cleanse the darkest dens of vice, misery, and sin. In ten years Shaftesbury wrought a striking transformation in the east end of London. Even the London *Times* confessed that not less than eighty thousand people had enjoyed the benefits of the reform. The author of "Municipal Government" tells us that Shaftesbury's lodging-houses furnish models for the world, and commend themselves to the philanthropists as the best method as yet devised for cleansing these bogs of misery and vice.

For children and youth cannot be pure within when all is darkness and filth without. When the company of Grecian youth went forth to found the city, and were injured by much draining of swamps and living in miasma, we are told the fairies came and in the night laid pipes for draining off the foul water, spanned the streams with bridges, changed the huts into houses, built temples and palaces on the public squares, surrounded all by a vast wall for their protection. But the story how fairies transformed a city of mud into one of marble seems as nothing compared to this man's transformation of these lands of misery, dirt and vice into a region characterized by comfort, cleanliness, and physical happiness for eighty thousand men and women.

One of the most interesting of Shaftesbury's reforms was his movement for the fifty thousand costermongers of London. The district in which they dwelt is one of mean streets, close alleys, gloomy tenements, being as barren of beauty or a green spot as a heap of sand or cinders. There little children toil, sweeping the filth from the streets; the men and women sell dried fish, fruit, old iron, pins, and needles. Not Stanley plunging through the tropic swamps and forests of Africa to investigate the sorrows of the dwarfs dwelling in the tree-tops, and the woes of those who suffered from the slave traffic was more persevering than was Shaftesbury in his investigations of the woes of the costermongers. Deeply interested in their welfare, he became their representative in Parliament, and succeeded in passing a bill in the interests of their district. He then bought a donkey and cart, and putting his name and coat-of-arms thereupon, he gave it to a poor girl to support her widowed mother. Then he organized a costers' fair, and founding a humane society in the interests of dumb beasts, each year he presented a prize donkey to the boy or man whose own beast showed the sign of having the best care.

For the twenty thousand children in the district he founded night schools, Sunday schools, and large industrial classes, with clubs for the men and women. One year the thousand boys planned a presentation to their benefactor, and uniting their pennies, purchased the finest donkey they could find in London. At the proper moment, when Shaftesbury was in the chair, the donkey, gayly decorated with ribbons and drawing the cart, with his name upon it, was led upon the platform and presented to Shaftesbury, while five thousand boys and their parents and friends stood upon chairs, and waving handkerchiefs, cheered wildly. In accepting the gift, with a touch of pathos, he said: "In closing my long life I desire only that it may be said of me that I have served men with a patience and resignation like unto this faithful beast."

Full speech over Shaftesbury's life and labor is impossible. Passing through a forest in October, the pilgrim may bear away a single golden bough, not all oaks or elms. It is not an easy task to call the roll of Shaftesbury's manifold labors. He gave fifteen years to collecting the facts and securing the passage of the lunacy bills that give the world our new system of asylums. He gave ten years to the factory towns of England, and passed bills that ameliorated the condition of three hundred thousand girls and women and secured the release from the looms of forty thousand children at two o'clock in the afternoon that they might spend three hours in the schoolroom. His industrial schools, ragged schools, shelter houses, loan associations for working-men, and his labor for chimney-sweeps occupied many more years. During this time he was also the co-worker and counselor of Cobden and John Bright in the corn-law movement.

It must also be remembered that twice he was a member of the cabinet, and for fifty years was one of the hardest worked men in Parliament. In his later years honors poured upon him like a flood. Deputations came to him with gifts from every part of the land. The whole nation did him honor when three hundred of the greatest men of England, including the statesmen, orators, scientists, scholars, and financiers, gave him an ovation at the Mansion House, and the mayor formally tendered him the freedom of the city of London. Almost daily some city sent a deputation to ask him to dedicate some library, gallery, hall, or inaugurate some public movement.

His last public duty was to visit Lord Salisbury with regard to the revelations in the *Pall Mall Gazette*. The next day he arose in the House of Lords and began a speech with the words: "My lords, I am now an old man. When I feel age creeping upon me and know I must soon die, I am deeply grieved, for I cannot bear to leave the world with so much misery in it." Overtaxed, that night he called for his daughter, and whispered: "Read me the words beginning, 'The Lord is my shepherd. Though I walk through the valley of the shadow of death, I will fear no evil.'" And while she read, a gentle smile came over his face, and the great man passed down that way o'er which none doth ever return.

Three days later a plain hearse, with four carriages, drove from his home toward Westminster Abbey. When the procession entered Pall Mall it became evident that all London was abroad to do the dead hero honor. The blinds were drawn in the great clubhouses and mansions, but the sidewalks and lanes were crowded with untold thousands. Reaching Trafalgar Square, forty thousand factory hands, seamstresses, flower girls, and laborers from the east end were found there assembled. Then came a mile through such crowds as London has scarcely ever seen. On either side of the street were deputations from the Sunday schools, the shelters, the homes, the training schools. When the hearse approached the costermongers, a leader lifted a banner with these words, "I was a stranger, and ye took me in." The boys from the ragged schools lifted this banner, "I was sick, and ye visited me." Upon a silken flag the leader of a thousand working girls had inscribed the words, "Inasmuch as ye did it unto one of the least of these, ye did it unto me." An hour later, in the great Abbey, were gathered royalty, lords, commons, city councils, the great merchants, financiers, and scholars of England. "This man goeth down to the grave," began the orator, "amid the benedictions of the poor and the admiring love of the rich." The next day, rising in Parliament, Lord Salisbury said: "My lords, the reforms of this century have been largely of England"; while Mr. Gladstone said, "The safety of our country is not in law or legislators, but in Christian gentlemen like unto Lord Shaftesbury."

X

The Biography of Frances Willard and the Heroes of Social Reform—A Study of the Knights of the New Chivalry

Social science affirms that woman's place in society marks the level of civilization. From its twilight in Greece, through the Italian worship of the Virgin, the dreams of chivalry, the justice of the civil law, and the equality of French society, we trace her gradual recognition; while our common law, as Lord Brougham confessed, was, with relation to women, the opprobrium of the age and of Christianity. For forty years plain men and women, working noiselessly, have washed away that opprobrium; the statute-books of thirty States have been remodeled, and woman stands to-day almost face to face with her last claim —the ballot. It has been a weary and thankless, though successful, struggle. But if there be any refuge from that ghastly curse—the vice of great cities, before which social science stands palsied and dumb—it is in this more equal recognition of woman. If, in this critical battle for universal suffrage—our fathers' noblest legacy to us, and the greatest trust God leaves in our hands—there will be any weapon, which once taken from the armory will make victory certain, it will be, as it has been in art, literature, and society, summoning woman into the political arena.— *Speeches and Lectures* (*Wendell Phillips*), *pp. 353, 354.*

X

THE BIOGRAPHY OF FRANCES WILLARD, AND THE HEROES OF SOCIAL REFORM—A STUDY OF THE KNIGHTS OF THE NEW CHIVALRY

Already an English, a French, and an American historian have told the story of the achievements of this closing half century. From different view-points these scholars have characterized our epoch as illustrious for what it has accomplished in politics, in war and wealth, in commerce and invention. But if our century has been a proud one for all lovers of their kind, its preëminence does not rest upon the increase of tools releasing the multitudes from drudgery; the increase of books releasing the multitudes from ignorance; the diffusion of art releasing the multitudes from ugliness; the development of science releasing the multitudes from squalor, pain, and suffering. When long time has passed by, historians will see that the crowning glory of our century has been the rise of the humanists and the development of a new order of chivalry.

For the first time in history the material forces of society have begun to be Christianized, and literature and wealth, position and eloquence, have allied themselves with the poor and the weak. No longer can rank bribe scholarship, or riches monopolize genius. In France our epoch has witnessed the rise of Victor Hugo's school, consecrating talent to the convicts and the poor of great cities. In England Charles Dickens pleads the cause of the orphan and the waif as typified by Oliver Twist and David Copperfield, while Kingsley, Besant, and Shaftesbury speak and write for the laborers in mines and factories. In our own land Harriet Beecher Stowe represents a multitude of writers who seek to ameliorate the lot of the slave and the outcast. The poets and essayists, also—Lowell and Whittier, Ruskin and Carlyle; those heroic soldiers named Gordon and Lord Lawrence, intrepid discoverers like Livingstone; living philanthropists and reformers, too, there are, whose names may not be mentioned, until death

hath starred them—these all have counted
themselves as retained by God in the interests of the weak and the downtrodden. If
in former centuries a single name like Dante
or Luther stands for an epoch, the hero being
like a star riding solitary through the night;
in our era the humanists and knights of
social reform are a great multitude—like
stars, indeed, for brightness and number,
and like stars, also, in that "God calleth
them all by name."

In all ages the reformers have gone the
way of contempt, obloquy, and shame, having their Gethsemane. From Paul to
Luther and Garrison and Gough, these men
have been the best hated men of their
times. In our fathers' day the very skies
rained lies and cruel slanders upon those
abolitionists who affirmed that the fugitive
slave law "was a compact with hell and a
league with the devil." But if in the lifetime of the reformers the fathers stoned the
prophets through the streets, covered their
garments with filth, mobbed their halls and
houses, the children are building monuments
to the reformer and teaching their sons the
pathway to the hero's tomb. "Time writes

the final epitaph,'' said Bacon; and we now see that those who in their lifetime allied themselves with the poor and weak have supremacy over the orators and statesmen and scholars who loved position and toiled for self.

In the interests of its children and youth, what would not this nation give to-day if Daniel Webster and Rufus Choate and Edward Everett had only refused compromise, stood unflinchingly for principle, and marched straight to that certain defeat in life that would have meant a certain victory after death? In the Pantheon of our immortals we now behold those intrepid reformers and radicalists who once vexed conservatism and annoyed the wealthy classes who loved ease, while the jurists and merchants and statesmen who sacrificed principle to selfish supremacy have received neither statue nor portrait, and have already passed into forgetfulness and obscurity.

But there in the sunlight stands, and shall stand forever, that Whittier, whose message was, indeed, sweetness and light, but who, when the fugitive slave law was passed, acted the hero's part, forged his thunderbolt, and wrote "Ichabod" across the brow of the erring statesman. There, too, is that elegant patrician, Wendell Phillips, the idol of Boston's most exclusive circle, the brilliant champion of luxury and conservatism, with his ambition for a place in the Senate, and supremacy for constitutional law, who proudly took his stand beside the slave, and knew that all the doors upon the avenues had closed behind him, and when his city jeered, hurled his polished epithets and scornful arrows upon the beautiful women and the cowardly men who once had been his companions. Nor must we forget Charles Sumner, with his knowledge of international law, his skill in diplomacy, and his ambition for foreign service, who gave up all his hopes and bound this motto as a frontlet between his eyes, "Bondage must be destroyed and liberty established," and who was at last knighted by the club of a coward, who smote him in the Senate chamber and brought the statesman to honor and immortality.

Here, too, is Garrison, serenely setting type for the *Liberator*, smiling scornfully upon the mob howling in the streets below his windows, even though destined an hour later to be dragged over the stones with a rope around his neck, and who in that hour was the only cool man in all the demoniac crowd. And here is Lowell, tuning his harp to songs of liberty; and Emerson from his study flinging cold, philosophical reflections into the very teeth of slavery; and here is Beecher with his flaming torch kindling the fires of liberty all over the land; and here is Douglass with his scars, speaking eloquently of the horrors of the slave market and the cotton field; and here is John Brown with smiling face and sunny heart going bravely to his martyrdom; and here also the company of noble women with their books and songs and stories strengthening the battle line. Nor must we forget Florence Nightingale with her crusade in the hospital and prison; Horace Mann with his crusade against ignorance; Gough with his crusade against intemperance; General Booth with his crusade for the neglected poor in great cities, and Livingstone toiling unceasingly through weary years to encircle the Dark Continent with lighthouses for mind and heart. The time was when these

reformers were despised, scoffed at, and
mobbed, with whose very names men would
not defile their lips. But now cities are
erecting their statues in the parks and building monuments in the public squares, that
children and youth may emulate their virtues. When time hath plowed our cities
into dust the names of these reformers and
heroes will survive as enduring monuments
to our age and civilization.

To those reformers who sought to destroy
slavery must now be added those who felt
that their task had only begun when the
physical fetters fell off, and so passed swiftly
on to achieve liberty for each enslaved mind
and heart. In Frances Willard our age has
lost one of its noblest daughters, whose
achievements for God and home and native
land were such as to rank her as one of the
most famous women of this century. Only
those who have lingered long over her books
and essays, or have passed under the full
spell of her luminous speech, or have considered her wide-reaching influence upon
our education, our civic institutions, can
understand why it is that two continents
mourn for our prophetess of self-renuncia-

tion. When Madame de Staël and George Eliot were borne to the tomb it could not be said of these daughters of genius that in a thousand towns and cities the multitudes assembled in church or hall to sit with bowed heads and saddened hearts, keeping a sacred tryst with memory during that solemn hour when afar off memorial words were being spoken above the silent dead. While she lived the American home seemed a little safer for her being here. What universal sorrow now that she hath gone!

If titled folk of foreign lands cabled sympathy and sent wreaths and flowers, the children of poverty and suffering also crowded the streets along that line of funeral march. The death of what private individual since Abraham Lincoln's time has called forth a thousand memorial funeral services upon the afternoon of one day? The time is not yet come for the analysis of Frances Willard's character, or the exhibition of her mental or moral traits. Among her divine gifts must be included a body firmly compacted and of unique endurance, yet delicately constituted as an Æolian harp; a voice sweet as a flute, yet heard of thousands; rare common sense, strength of reason and memory, singular insight into human nature, intuitive knowledge of public men and measures; tact, sympathy, imagination, enthusiasm, with a genius for sacrifice and self-renunciation. Early successful as an authoress, highly honored with position and rank in the realm of higher education, she turned her back upon all offers of promotion.

She organized a work for women through women, her brain conceiving the new thought, her heart lending it momentum, her will executing the vast conception. In the beginning she toiled without salary, until she had expended her little store, and came to such straits that, for want of carfare she had to walk to and from her dark, bare office. Soon she set before herself the task of addressing the people in every city in our land that had ten thousand people. When twelve years had passed by she had stood before four thousand audiences, a feat surpassed only by Beecher, Gough, and Moody. She was largely instrumental in securing the enactment of laws in all the States of the Union, save Texas, Arkansas, and Virginia, to introduce physiological temperance and the scientific study of stimulants and narcotics into the curriculum of the common school. For years she was misunderstood; oft was she cruelly criticised, full oft despised and scorned. But at last she has fulfilled her career. She is now with Augusta Stanley and Mary Lyon, with Lucretia Mott and Harriet Beecher Stowe. Having met them and received their approval, what cares she for our praise? As was said of Wendell Phillips, so is it of supreme importance to us and our children that Frances Willard should think well of us.* Whom God hath crowned, let us remember, man may not discrown.

Not until our children's children come to write the history of the reform movement of this century can the influence of the noble women who have toiled for temperance be rightly understood. Nevertheless, if we contrast the drinking habits and customs of the former generation with those of our own era we shall obtain some conception of the enormous gains made in national so-

* P. 597, Oration on Wendell Phillips, in " Modern Perils and Opportunities."—Joseph Cook.

briety. If to-day in Frances Willard's home, in Evanston, the children and youth of ninety-five homes out of each hundred have never known the taste of spirits, at the beginning of this century drunkenness was well-nigh universal. But eighty years have passed by since Lyman Beecher said: "Rum consecrates our baptisms, our weddings, and our funerals. Our vices are digging the grave of our liberties." About the same time, when a prominent merchant of Philadelphia died, and his pastor went to the house to the funeral, he found the table under the trees was spread with liquor, in which the people were freely indulging. The writer affirms that on reaching the grave, save himself and the grave-digger, there was not a man present who was not in danger, through intoxication, of falling into the grave. Even as late as 1826 the ministerial associations of Rhode Island and Connecticut provided wine and liquor for the annual meeting of the clergy.

And once the great temperance movement was inaugurated, it began as regulation, and not as prohibition. The earliest printed temperance pledge that has come down to us includes two clauses: (1) No member shall drink rum, under penalty of twenty-five cents. (2) No member shall be intoxicated, under penalty of fifty cents. When total abstinence was proposed men received it with scorn and jeers, and the total abstainer became almost an outcast. When one of the early founders of a temperance society in Vermont refused liquor to the neighbors who were helping him raise his new barn, his friends dropped their tools and refused their service, and although the total abstainer scoured the township for helpers, he was unable to obtain laborers until he furnished the usual liquors. Angry at this temperance fanatic, one old gentleman exclaimed: "How bigoted is this abstainer; unless checked such fanaticism will ruin the country and break up the Democratic party"—which must not be interpreted as meaning that the Republicans drank less heavily. At last Dr. Cheever wrote his celebrated tract on "Deacon Giles' Distillery." Using another name, he described the career of one Deacon Story, who to his business as a distiller added the duties of agent of the Bible society, selling bottles from one counter and Bibles from the other, into whose malt vat one day his drunken son fell and was drowned. When the distiller read his but thinly disguised biography in Dr. Cheever's book, he arrested the scholar for libel and threw him into jail. The public discussion that followed fell upon the public mind like a spark upon the Western prairies, and soon the whole land was aglow with the greatest temperance movement known to history.

Then, just at the critical moment, God raised up Gough to trouble the hosts of intemperance. At first this reformed book-binder stood forth as a color-bearer, leading the hosts forward, but soon his flag-staff was found to have a spear at the end of it. Without the polished scholarship of Edward Everett, without the elegant grace and charm of Wendell Phillips, without the universal genius of Beecher, this reformer brought to his task a certain inborn impulsive, magnetic, all-enkindling eloquence, that defies analysis, yet for platform work has certainly never been surpassed, perhaps never equaled. Once in a century it is given to a great actor like Irving to

put some play of Shakespeare on the stage
ninety nights in succession. But Gough
entered Exeter Hall in London, and for
ninety successive nights, with ever-chang-
ing lecture, crowded that vast amphitheater
to the streets with merchants, bankers,
scholars, with outcasts and drunkards. His
voice was a noble instrument of many keys;
his eyes were large and liquid, overflowing
with kindness, sympathy and good humor;
he had a dramatic delivery and power of
imitation that were of the highest order;
with unrivaled skill he poured forth anec-
dotes, witticisms, pathetic stories, and arguments, also, that were merciless in their
logic and all-convincing in their conclusions.
For two hours each evening we have seen
him walk from one end of the platform to
the other, so that the hearer might ask the
question, asked of an old Roman orator,
"How many miles have you talked to-
night?"

In forty years he addressed fourteen
thousand audiences, averaging one thousand hearers each, and traveled more miles
on his lecture tours than would reach twenty
times around the globe. Yet by keeping

close to God's heart and the people, he
went on gaining in freshness to the very
end. At last standing before a vast audience in Philadelphia, he lifted his hand,
and with an impressive gesture, said: "I
have seven years in the record of my life
when I was held in the iron grasp of intemperance. I would give the world to blot it
out; but alas! I cannot." Then with flaming face and uplifted eyes, he exclaimed,
"Therefore, young men, make your record
clean." And because God would have
these words ever before America's youth,
upon the instant came the final imperious
summons, and he fell like a soldier, face to
face with his foe, and knighted in the very
thick of his battle.

If God oft withdraws His leaders, He
makes His work go on. The period of emo-
tional excitement and national enthusiasm
was now to pass into a period of organiza-
tion and legislative enactment. At a critical moment a gifted woman came forward
to organize a work for women through
women. Not but that Frances Willard was
an orator as well as an organizer. Doubtless those who dwell in great cities and have

only heard her speak in great halls holding two or three thousand people can have little conception of her genius for public speech. In the very nature of the case she did not have a voice like Webster or Beecher, whose tones in times of great excitement made the windows to rattle, while some said, "It thunders."

Her greatest oratorical triumphs were in villages and cities where some hall holding not more than a thousand people was crowded with appreciative listeners. At such times she stood forth one of the most gifted speakers of this generation, achieving effects that were truly amazing. What ease and grace of bearing! What gentleness and strength! What pathos and sympathy! How exquisitely modulated her words! If her speech did not flow as a gulf stream, if it did not beat like an ocean upon a continent, she sent her sentences forth, an arrowy flight, and each "tipped with divine fire." Those students of great orators who have lingered long over the masterpieces of politics and reform are those who have most admired the oratorical method Frances Willard developed upon the platform. What a world of meaning she crowded into some of her epigrams, like "The golden rule of Christ will bring the golden age to man." When the distinguished philanthropists and reformers and citizens of England assembled in the City Temple of London to give her a reception, and heaped upon her the highest honors, those of us who listened to her response knew that her reserves of character were vast indeed. With what simplicity and modesty did she decline all praise, insisting that she received these honors simply in the name of the women of America, for whom England intended them.

In that time of strained political relations between the two nations, with what fine patriotism did she speak of her flag, saying: "I am first a Christian, then I am a Saxon, then I am an American, and when I get home to Heaven, I expect to register from Evanston." To organize a great political machine that represents the Republican or Democratic party, where cities and counties and states are all related as wheel to wheel, requires the skill of tens of thousands of expert politicians, toiling ceaselessly. But beginning with nothing, in twenty years, single-handed, this woman organized the women of her country into a vast mechanism that extended to village and city and state and nation, and to foreign lands, with machinery for public agitation, a system of temperance journals for children and youth, for securing instruction upon the nature of stimulants in the common schools, with more than sixty different departments and methods of activity. It has been said that the measure of a career is determined by three things: First, the talent that ancestry gives; second, the opportunity that events offer; third, the movements that the mind and will conceive and compel. Doubtless for Frances Willard ancestry bestowed rare gifts, the opportunity was unique, but that which her mind and heart compelled is beyond all measurement. As in times past orators have used the names Howard and Nightingale for winging their words, for all the ages to come editors and publicists and speakers will hold up the name of Willard for the stimulus and inspiration of generations yet unborn.

Sometimes our temperance reformers are

counted harsh in speech, critical in temper,
of narrow view-point, lacking in generosity
and sanity of judgment. But broad minds
will also be just and generous, even toward
those who are thought to be extremists.
The very heart of the temperance reform is
this single principle: Those strong and well-
poised persons who will never be injured
by the use of wine owe something to the
weak ones who will be destroyed thereby.
When for three generations a family uses
liquor in excess, nature registers the deterioration. His biographer tells us that the first
Webster represented colossal strength and
sobriety. This giant had a son, Daniel,
who represented colossal strength and moderate drinking, while his son represented
erratic strength, and his grandson represented
one who made the amusements of his ances-
tors to be his occupation. Often ancestry explains these who are born with soft nerve
and flabby brain, and, like the reed, bow
before the wind of temptation. And the
strong owe them sympathy, shelter, and
protection. Our age is still cruel and harsh
toward the children of weakness and temptation. Our alleys and tenement-houses are

filled with the children of ignorance and squalor, who have been cursed by centuries of misrule and superstition under foreign governments, who were born without nerve or poise or self-control. And for the state to place stimulants in their hand is for a parent to give pistols, razors, and bomb-shells to babes to use as playthings.

Every year our nation expends $1,100,-000,000 for liquor, about $10,000,000 for art, and $10,000,000 for literature, and $5,000,000 for missions and the ameliora-tion of the poor. The wastes through intemperance in one American city alone in ten years equal the destruction of two Chi-cago fires. Could the children of poverty in Chicago be induced to give up their whisky and beer for the next ten years, the saving would develop a playground for chil-dren in the center of every ward, develop gymnasiums and bath-houses equal to those of the Greeks and Romans, erect a Parthenon enriched with the pictures and statues of the great men of history, build and equip twenty manual training schools equal to the largest in our city, erect ten art institutes, representing the treasures of our museum.

Frances Willard

To all young men and maidens comes the reflection that all the splendid gifts named talent, beauty, wealth, and position have their crowning glory when used for the poor and weak. The lives of the heroes and reformers tell us that supremacy does not come through running with the currents or flattering the great in the interests of position, or falling in with the multitude that the tides of public favor may sweep one on to fame and fortune. To-day to many a youth tempted to ease and prosperity and dreams of ambition comes the silent voice of conscience and of Christ, bidding him adhere to principle, not policy, and service rather than selfishness, and burden-bearing rather than ease and luxury. And to many a girl to-day, with her beauty and culture and gifts that prophesy rare social success, will come the sirens singing of ease and luxury and position.

And in the hour of her temptation she will sin against her higher ideals, marry downward instead of upward, choose a nest that is soft and silken, to find long afterward that the palace of luxury is none other than a prison; only when the years have gone, suddenly to meet one standing in the way like unto the angel of God, whom God intended as true mate, and then, behold! life is but dust and ashes! Oh, life is full of piteous tragedies! What hells in kings' houses! What heavens in garrets! What bond-slaves of poverty as well as luxury! What princesses are these named "The Sisters of the Poor"! How does happiness bubble like a spring in the heart of these heroes who turn their back upon the blandishments of position and place, and where others have said, "The devil take the hindmost," have said, "I will take the hindmost"! Oh, happy, thrice happy, shall we be if in that day of revelation some one once wounded like a bird stands forth, some one once stormed and in sore need of a harbor and refuge, some of Christ's little ones, once scarred and battered with their sins, shall rise up and with shining face say, "Master, I was sick, I was in prison, I was an hungered, and this one, Thy disciple, ministered unto me"! There, that radiant word shall repay you a thousand times for the obloquy, defeat, scorn, and misfortunes that always have been heaped upon Christ's heroes and reformers.

XI

Blaikie's "Personal Life of David Livingstone"—A Study of Nineteenth-Century Heroism

When profane history spreads out before you the bloody page of Alexander, and Cæsar, and Nero, and your heart feels faint and sick, turn away and look upon these missionary faces that have gone from earth to heaven, and your eyes will dim with tears of gratitude that God made man so noble in feelings and in destiny. Guizot and Hallam and all the philosophers of history tell us what good influences came from the knights-errant that wandered for a few generations over Europe. We are assured that they rode to and fro with helmet and sword and armor in the interest of equity. It is possible that they developed military prowess and some new conception of personal honor. But whenever the world's civilization shall desire to see the heroes that laid the deep foundations of our age and the coming more golden time, it will have to pass by the glittering mail of knights and see the Pauls, and Marquettes, and Elliotts, and Duffs moving around wearing the sword of the Spirit and the richly jeweled helmet of salvation.

O, the loftiest spirit of earth, the soul of a Paul, or a Xavier, or a Livingstone. It is said that men throw their offerings down at the feet of the gods because the human eye is unable to see and the human arm too short to enable the worshiper to place his garlands upon the forehead of Deity. With similar weakness and humility we all, of a mercenary and infidel age, being unable to see and reach the divine forehead of this missionary spirit, that loftiest shape of soul, cannot do otherwise than come to-day and whisper our words of homage at her feet.—*Truths for To-day, pp. 191, 192, 193.*

XI

BLAIKIE'S "PERSONAL LIFE OF DAVID LIVINGSTONE"—A STUDY OF NINE-TEENTH-CENTURY HEROISM

From the beginning of time man has been a lover of bravery and a worshiper of heroes. Tales of eloquence are interesting, but stories of courage have always seemed the most fascinating books in libraries. For the most part the heroes of liberty, phil-anthropy, and religion have gone through life in a garb of self-sacrifice and modesty, but once the great man is fully revealed society hastens to break its alabaster box upon his forehead and bathes his feet with admiring tears. Of old, men traced Cæsar's march through Gaul by the villages he de-stroyed and the fields he devastated; but we trace the heroes' progress through the cen-turies by the wastes that have become gar-dens and the deserts that now are Edens. Indeed, the history of society is very largely the history of a handful of heroes, who have died perhaps in the desert or on the battlefield, but who in dying bequeathed a republic to followers who had been serfs or slaves.

If we call the roll of all the great achievements for mankind, the extinction of gladiatorial games, the trial of witnesses by fire prohibited, the bonds of serfs broken, the exposure of children forbidden, the doing away with the wrecker's rights, we shall find that each new victory for our race begins with some valiant leader who died for his book of reform or philanthropy. But such is the hero's power that his spirit cannot be holden, even of death itself. Standing in the clouds of heaven, the ascended poet or leader, soldier or saint, rains down inspiration upon the multitude, and soon lifts the whole people to his level. Once death clears the clouds from some great soul named Socrates or Savonarola, Luther or Livingstone, the people follow after his example, as once the Roman multitude followed the chariot of some conqueror. Man does well to worship his heroes, for these are they who have lifted the gates of the prisons from their hinges, broken the

swords of tyrants, and led the pilgrim hosts
into "the promised land" of learning and
liberty.

To our pleasure-loving generation comes
the career of David Livingstone, telling us
that the age of heroism has not ended and
must not end. If for the countless millions
of the Dark Continent Livingstone's legend
has become a "pillar of cloud by day and a
pillar of fire by night," leading them out of
the bondage and the wilderness, his influence upon civilized nations has been scarcely
less, rebuking our ease and smiting self-indulgence. For courage in Livingstone was
as high and fine as in Sir Galahad of old.
Heroism was in his blood like iron, in his
eye like fire, in his voice like the trum-
pet call. This man, who flung himself upon
the African slave traffic, and single-handed
determined to give a continent to commerce
and Christianity—this scarred hero differs
from our perfumed effeminates as an iron-
clad differs from a pleasure yacht, as a
piece of iron from a painted lath, as Cromwell differs from some Beau Brummell.
History holds no career so strangely
marked by heroic adventure and hairbreadth

escapes, perils in jungle and perils in swamp,
perils of the lion's stroke and the serpent's
bite, perils of war-clubs and poisoned arrows, perils of dwarfs in forests and strong
men in the hill country. In 1842, when
Livingstone first landed upon the African
coast and determined to penetrate the very
heart of the Dark Continent, Africa was
the land of horrors and of mystery, known
only to the traders who penetrated the
edge of the forest to trap slaves for Cuban
plantations. Since then no other continent has experienced changes so wide-
reaching as this country, now known as the
land of gold and gems, the land of ivory,
pearls, and perfumes, the land of amber,
spices, and rich woods, the land of the
black races, where God has chiseled His
"image in ebony."

To-day, obedient to Livingstone's call for
staying the ravages of the slave traffic,
Europe is carving Africa into free states.
Explorers are perfecting their maps of rivers,
mountains, and plains. Merchants are
traversing the country with roads and rail-
ways. Statesmen are enacting laws that
shall abolish the last vestige of the traffic in

men. The tragedy of Gordon at Khartoum, the intrepid explorations of Stanley, the fame of gold fields of the Cape and diamond fields of Kimberley, have made the whole world aware of the marvels of this rich continent. If the nineteenth century has made the black slave a free man, the twentieth century bids fair to make the Dark Continent the land of light and liberty. And this wonderland is practically Livingstone's gift to civilization. His twenty-nine thousand miles of discovery and exploration added one million square miles to the known world. His studies of Africa's geology, botany, and zoölogy won for him the highest honors that scientific societies could bestow. His writings upon African flora and fauna won for him the esteem of the world's then greatest scientists, like Owen, Murchison, and Herschel. His studies of the African languages lent him fame among philologists. With Sir Bartle Frere let us confess that in ages to come he will be known as a hero—one of the bravest men in history, being to the Dark Continent what Lincoln was to our own country.

Fascinating indeed the childhood and

youth of this hero, whose character and career make it hard to disbelieve in the divine origin of the Christianity that molded him. He was of Scotland's sturdiest stock, and was hammered out upon the anvil of adversity. The courage and spirit of Robert Bruce and his heroic clansmen were in this Highland son, and in later years were seen a thousand times in moments when Livingstone marched into the camp of armed warriors, and without a single fear lay down to sleep in the midst of these painted savages. Not wealth nor ease, leisure nor social rank equipped him; adversity chose him for her knight. The child of poverty, at ten years of age he entered the factory, where six o'clock in the morning found his little fingers guiding the thread, and when the evening darkness fell he was still standing beside the loom. The first half-crown he earned went for a Latin grammar, which he fastened to the frame of his wheel, while between the revolutions he snatched a moment for his nouns and verbs. At sixteen he finished his Virgil, Horace, and Cicero, and best of all had formed those habits of patient and accurate research that

long continued made him at last a ripe
scholar. Taking up the study of history,
politics, and literature, he became interested
in the ministry, and made his way to Glasgow, where he hired a garret, cooked his
oatmeal and studied, made a little tea and
studied, went forth to walk, but studied
ever. Interested in the classics, he laid the
foundations for his study of the dialects of
Africa. An eager student of the sciences,
he fitted himself for his researches in geology, geography, and botany. Later he
entered the medical college, and studied
surgery, achieving the skill that made him
seem to the Africans a divine healer. Then
he went up to London, and there pursued
his researches in philosophy, theology, and
ethics.

At the moment when he was ordained to
the ministry the opium war was dragging on
in China, and he determined to make his
way to the Celestial kingdom. But in that
hour he met Moffat, newly arrived from
Africa, who argued that the Dark Continent
needed some one who had the courage to
leave the coast and march straight into the
interior, where on a clear morning, from a

mountain-top, the traveler might see smoke rising from a thousand villages in which no foreigner had ever stood. But the danger of African fever or of death by the natives, the danger of sunstroke was so great that the board would not assign him to Africa. In the hour of his insistence the directors gave their consent, but disclaimed all responsibility for the perilous undertaking. Learning that the South African steamer was to sail almost immediately, Livingstone hurried home to bid his parents farewell. Arriving at evening, all night long father and mother and son sat talking of the perils and possibilities of the Dark Continent, and when the morning light crept over the hills the son read the words, "Thou shalt not be afraid of the terror by night, nor of the arrow that flieth by day." Then began the walk to Glasgow. On the hilltop hard by, father and son looked into each other's faces for the last time. Then Livingstone set his face toward the Dark Continent, little dreaming that the time would come when the Glasgow whose shores he was leaving would give him tumultuous welcome home, cover him with medals and resolutions, and bestow the freedom of the city upon her most distinguished citizen.

If Florence Nightingale speaks of David Livingstone as "the most remarkable man of his generation," the events of his early career in South Africa seem to fully justify the judgment. Landing at the Cape, with characteristic courage the young hero plunged at once into the forest and secluded himself from all but the natives, that he might master the language, habits, and ideas of the people. At the end of seven months he reappeared upon the coast, able to converse with African chiefs with perfect ease. In his enthusiasm he began collecting provisions for a tour of a thousand miles into the interior. Then for six months he marched north toward the heart of Africa. But at the moment when scores of unfriendly tribes were between him and his friends upon the coast, his oxen died, and he was obliged to desert his supplies. In that hour he packed his luggage and trudged on, keeping only his medicines and remedies.

Entering some village that had never seen the face of a white man, he would march with erect fearlessness through the ranks of warriors, and with a genial smile and outstretched hand boldly enter the tent of the chief. His courageous manner, gentle address, and kindly spirit seemed to cast a spell upon all hearts, and he soon received not simply protection, but even reverence and homage from those whom Boers and Arabs called treacherous and wily imps and devils. Yet in years not one single article was stolen from him, and because his presence was a boon to the people he was treated as a kind of superior being. His fame began as a rainmaker. Assembling the native chiefs, he led them to the head of a rich valley that had been overtaken by drought, and there outlined a plan of irrigation with canals and reservoirs. When a year had passed—lo, the little valley was a garden of beauty and delight. Sending to the coast for a dozen tool chests, he taught the people carpentering, the building of houses and barns, and the making of wagons. He started an agricultural school, and developed vineyards and orchards, and taught the grafting of fruits, the raising of grains, and the care of stock. He enrolled two hundred women in an industrial school, where his wife taught dressmaking and housekeeping, while he taught the use of foods, the care of the eyes and ears and the general health, with remedies for diseases of childhood.

When the first Christian missionary landed in England in 590, he found our Saxon forefathers were cannibals, wearing coats of skin, worshiping charms, and eating the flesh of enemies slain in battle. But nine hundred years of Christian instruction ushered in the era of Shakespeare. In like manner Livingstone's ideal was to teach as a Christian gentleman with a typical English home. When seven years had passed by he beheld a transformation how marvelous. He built a house, and straightway the chief erected a home like it. He filled a space in front of his home with flowerbeds; soon all the tents were surrounded with brilliant blossoms. He assembled the children and youth on Sunday morning for instruction, and the chief sent out servants with whips of rhinoceros skin and drove in five hundred young men, that Livingstone might instruct them. His days were filled with husbandry, wagon-making, stock-raising, while his evenings were occupied with the instruction of twenty-five young men whom he was training to carry on his work. It was here, too, that he had his famous adventure with the lion, and suffered that injury to his arm that made possible the identification of his body when his faithful Susa brought the bones to London.

One autumn the cattle suffered severely through the midnight attack of lions, and Livingstone planned to make a circuit about the herd in the hope of driving the wild beasts toward the center. In the morning, moving through the high grass, he came suddenly upon a beast that sprang full upon him and brought him to the ground. "He caught me by the shoulder," writes Livingstone, "and shook me as I have seen a terrier shake a rat. The shock produced a stupor like that produced to a mouse in the grip of a cat. It caused a sense of dreaminess." He says he was quite conscious of all that was happening. "It was like a patient under the influence of chloroform, who is conscious of the operation, but does not feel the knife, perhaps a merciful provision of the Creator for lessening the pain of death.'' A moment later the beast in the agony of death dropped the arm, its bones crushed, the flesh in shreds. But the slave-dealers, who feared him, were more cruel than wild beasts. Returning from the coast, where he had gone to send his family home to England, he found that the Boers had sacked the villages, burned all his buildings, destroyed his tents and vines, and scattered his people. Then it was that he determined to launch a crusade against the traffic in human flesh, and bring the Portuguese and Spanish slavers before the court of the world.

The wanderings of Ulysses are not more fascinating than this epoch of discovery and exploration that now began for Livingstone. With no guide but his compass, he determined to plunge into the interior and cross the Dark Continent, hoping to come out somewhere near the mouth of the Congo River. Warned that this was a forlorn hope, he wrote a letter home to England, saying: ''I shall open up a path through this continent or perish. My blessings on my wife. May God comfort her. If I never return, my Paris medal goes to

Thomaa, my sextant to Robert.'' Then,
having no supporters, like Stanley or Sir
Samuel Baker, having no guides, no maps,
no army of aids, he plunged into the forest
to follow the stars and be guided by his compass and astronomical instruments. His bag-
gage, carried by natives, consisted of twenty
pounds of coffee and a like amount of tea.
For his food he depended upon his gun and
three muskets for natives. He also had
three tin boxes, each fifteen inches square,
one filled with beads, one with clothing,
and one with medicines. To this scant
equipment he added a tent, which was just
large enough to shield him from the rain
when lying down. The perils that he endured during the five years in the wilderness
well-nigh surpass belief. He found the vast
tropic jungle one tangled maze well-nigh
impenetrable, with trees one hundred and
fifty feet high, shutting out the sun by day
and making the darkness by night well-nigh
palpable. The rich and reeking soil sent
up an undergrowth of thorns and briers that
tore the flesh, while stinging nettles were
often waist-deep. Rain also fell every other
day for months, and he scarcely knew what

it was to have dry feet or garments. He waded and swam hundreds of streams and rivers. Once, tying logs together for a raft, a hippopotamus attacked it and threw Livingstone into the river. Lying down to sleep, a lion sprang upon two of his men and slew them. He was bitten by serpents, and twice his life hung in the balance.

Once mistaken for a slave-driver, he came near having his brains beaten out with war-clubs. Another time he found himself alone in the midst of a mob of armed savages. Amusing them with his watch, compass, and sextant, he backed to the river bank, got into a log canoe that he had made, and holding up his magic lantern for them to look at got across the stream and found his men again. He traveled for three hundred miles through a swampy region, where the marsh gases threatened his life. In two years he suffered twenty-seven attacks of African fever, lasting from one to three weeks. The result was that during the last three hundred miles of his journey he was so dizzy that he could not hold his instrument steady nor perform a single calculation, nor tell the time of day nor the day of the week. At last his faithful men tied him upon an ox that they led slowly forward. When Xenophon's soldiers, in the retreat of the Ten Thousand, saw the sea, they joyfully exclaimed: "The sea! The sea!" But when Livingstone's servants emerged from the dark forest the traveler was scarcely conscious enough to understand the scene, and his faithful men having never seen the ocean, knelt about him in their alarm and said, "The world says, 'I am finished. There is no more of me.'" Worn to a skeleton, scarcely able to understand his deliverance, for weeks Livingstone lay in the home of the consul, battling with the African fever and struggling back to life.

Then he set himself to the task of completing his maps and charts containing the notes as to the width and depth of rivers and streams, the direction of their flow, and the country they drained; accounts of the forests, the various woods and grains, and also perfected his geological, botanical, and zoölogical notes. When his task was nearing completion an English steamer anchored near shore, and the captain offered Livingstone passage home, where friends and fame awaited him. But Livingstone had promised his natives that if they would be true to him he would return them to their friends in safety. And so, putting away all thoughts of home and love, he turned back again for a journey of two thousand miles straight across Africa from west to east, being destined to discover the Victoria Falls, and to undergo sufferings and adventures such as have characterized the career of no discoverer in history. Having brought his servants home again, he journeyed on to Juimaline, where he arrived in August, 1857, after five years of solitude in the forests, and so set sail for home, where he was destined to find himself the most famous man then in the British Isles.

A modest man and reticent, Livingstone's welcome home brought surprise that was bewilderment. The Royal Geographical Society received him, and in its name Sir Robert Murchison presented him with a gold medal. London hastened to do him honor, and assembling its statesmen, lords, scientists, merchants, the lord mayor presented him with the freedom of the city. Glasgow welcomed him home with a public reception, and her dignitaries presented Livingstone with an address and a gold box containing ten thousand dollars in coin. Edinburgh, Liverpool, Dublin, Manchester, and a score of other cities and towns voted him public honors and rich gifts. The universities of Oxford and Cambridge bestowed honorary degrees, as did Dublin, Glasgow, and Paris. Addressing the Commercial Club of London, he exhibited to her merchants and manufacturers specimens of twenty-five kinds of dried fruits, showed them oils of which they had never heard, native dyes hitherto unknown, fibers for making paper, told them of sheep that had hair instead of wool, exhibited specimens of African honey, sugar-cane, millet, wheat, cotton, iron, and coal. He insisted that it was of capital importance to England to open up a railway into what we now know as the Lake Nyassa region, where to-day England is building a railway one thousand miles long.

Indeed, Livingstone was the lion of the year, and his popularity was such as to eclipse the fame of England's greatest leaders. But this modest traveler, naturalist, scientist, physician, missionary, soon withdrew from public life, and secluding himself in the old home in Scotland, wrote out his "Missionary Travels," in the hope of securing funds for another expedition. "For," said he, in the outset of his book, "so far as my calling is concerned, the end of the geographical feat is only the beginning of my missionary enterprise." For having secured a knowledge of the country and freedom for the body of slaves, his Christian spirit rushed on to include Christ's freedom for the mind and heart. The first edition of twelve thousand volumes of his book was sold for one guinea, and was taken within a single week. Finding the amount sufficient to provide for his new expedition, he immediately set sail for Africa, unspoiled by honors such as England has bestowed upon but two or three men of this century. Landing at Zanzibar, he went immediately into the interior, and made a circle of a thousand miles, collecting facts that secured governmental interference with the Portuguese slave traffic, discovering and exploring the sources of the River Zambesi, Lake Nyassa, and finding the key to the river system that explained the headwaters of the Nile. Upon his return to the coast he found his wife ill with African fever, unconscious, and dying. Three months later an expedition arrived from the coast, and its leader found that the hero who had faced so many dangers, braved so many deaths, had at last lost all heart and hope, for he had buried his life with Mary Livingstone at the foot of a great babbah tree. When another broken and sad year had passed in travel, he determined to return to England, publish the record of his five years of travel, sell the manuscript, arrange for his sons' future, and set sail for Africa, to make one last attempt to discover the headwaters of the Nile.

Within a year after his return to Africa Livingstone was a thousand miles in the interior, in the midst of tribes that had never seen a white face. Twenty-five years of exposure and privation had sorely taxed his strength, but he adhered unflinchingly to his determination to make a desperate effort to get at the centers of the slave trade, collect information sufficient to justify a congress of the powers for concerted action against the traffic in men, and also, if possible, discover the sources of the Nile. When Christmas Day of 1867 came he was so weak as to be reduced to a diet of milk, and on New Year's day his goats were stolen and his one luxury gone. "Took up my belt three holes to relieve hunger," was his entry New Year's day of 1868. Then for three months, ill with rheumatic fever, he lay in a rude hut that his men built for him. One day he saw the wild bees entering a hollow tree, and writes: "It is now two years since I have tasted sugar or honey." Traveling slowly through the forest he came across a little mound beneath a great tree, and musing there, writes: "I have nothing to do but to trudge on, until He who has brought me safe thus far bids me lie down beneath His trees to die."

The following year he discovered and explored Lake Noero and Lake Bankweolo, and from the formation of the country developed the theory that in the great lakes of the north, of which the natives had told him, he would find the headwaters of the Nile—a theory that later proved to be true. "If I have life," writes the old hero, "I will yet make sure of it." Then he renewed his travels northward, trudging slowly, for he was weary in mind and body. Unfortunately he was doomed to suffer through the treachery of the slave-dealers. Returning to the village where two years before he had left his supplies, he found that all his stores had been destroyed, not even one dose of quinine remaining. It was in November of 1871, while striving to collect himself from the shock of finding that he was without money, beads, calico, or goods to hire the men for completing his work, that his faithful Susa came crying: "Master, a white man comes." A moment later, leaning on his staff for very weakness, Livingstone grasped the hand of Stanley, who had been sent by the *New York Herald* to find Livingstone if living, and if dead to bring home his bones. That night his journal includes these words: "The news I have heard from Europe makes my whole frame thrill. What a terrible fate has befallen France at Sedan. The ocean cable successfully laid in the Atlantic, the election of General Grant as President, the death of Lord Clarendon. The voting of a thousand pounds by Parliament for supplies to help my work has put new life into me." For four months these two men wrought together, the one a veteran who had borne the burden and heat of the day, the other a young knight who had but just won his golden spurs. One fact was certain, the atmosphere of Livingstone transformed the spirit, ambition, motives, and character of Stanley.

The young traveler at length came to look upon Livingstone as one who deserved homage and worship. What a portrait is that he paints of Livingstone! "His gentleness never forsakes him, his hopefulness never deserts. No harassing anxieties can make him complain. To the stern dictates of duty alone has he sacrificed home and ease, the pleasures, refinements, and luxuries of civilized life. His is the Spartan heroism, the inflexibility of the Roman, the enduring resolution of the Anglo-Saxon— never to surrender his obligations until he can write 'finis' to his work. His religion has made him the most companionable of men and indulgent of masters. Each Sunday morning he gathers his little flock about

him and reads prayers and a chapter from
the Bible, and delivers a short address in a
natural, unaffected, and sincere tone. The
natives passing Livingstone exclaim, 'The
blessing of God rest on you.' '' Despite
every argument that Stanley could use for
Livingstone to return home, the hero
refused to give up his unfulfilled purpose.
Stanley urged the claims of home and
friends, what a reception awaited him in
England and America, what cheers from
great societies and savants, what opportunity to establish missions and commerce and
suppress the slave traffic! One morning at
four o'clock David Livingstone arose and
gave into Stanley's hands his journal, maps,
charts, and notes that made the interior of
Africa a known country, and with the single
word "God bless you," the quiet, reserved
missionary of Jesus Christ turned back toward the forest, while Stanley went away
to end his record of travel with the words:
"For four months and four days I lived with
Livingstone, and I never found a fault in
him. Each day's life only added to my
admiration."

Pathetic indeed the events of the few

months after the departure of Stanley. For
several months Livingstone toiled on, racked
with unspeakable pain, able to take nothing
except goat's milk. It was the rainy season, and he was worn with fever and rheu-
matism; yet each day he traveled a few
miles down the river bank, exploring on
every side for indications of a slope toward
the north. In April he writes: "I am very
weak from bleeding through a vein that
keeps breaking and saps away my strength."
Too weak to use his instruments after the
day's march, his men now carried him forward on a litter, for he was determined to
press on. One afternoon he bade the men
camp early, and seemed to be wandering in
his mind. Midst the drizzling rain a rude
hut was hastily constructed. In the night
the boy who lay at the door of the tent
called for Susa, saying that the master was
ill and so still that he was afraid. Entering
the tent they found Livingstone kneeling,
his head buried in his hands upon the pillow. He had gone on his last long journey,
and no man was with him. But he had
died praying for Africa—for Africa and all
her woes and sins and wrongs, to the

Avenger of the oppressed and the Redeemer of the lost. In his journal were these words: "All I can say in my solitude is, may Heaven's rich blessing come down on every one—American, English, Turk—who will help to heal this open sore of the world."

Could Livingstone have known of the courage, affection, and loyalty that his black servants were to manifest after his death, that knowledge alone would have repaid him for thirty years in the African wastes. With instant resolution, his faithful friends determined to carry his body and his books to England. They buried the heart at the base of a great tree, on which they carved his name. Having dried the body in the sun, they wrapped it in calico, and started to the coast. It was a journey of nine months through unfriendly tribes and an unknown region, midst dangers that conquered the admiration of the world. In the retreat of the Ten Thousand, the Greek soldiers marched home, and were encouraged by the love and welcome of men who were living. Xenophon's men also were Greeks—soldiers, armed and educated. But these

negroes had been slaves, their Livingstone
was dead, and they endured innumerable
dangers without any hope of reward. From
Zanzibar his bones, still guarded by his
faithful Susa, were sent to England, where
they were met by a special train. Sir William Ferguson identified the body immediately by the false joint in the arm. The
heart of all England swelled with grief and
pride over one of her noblest sons. In the
presence of an immense concourse, England's greatest scientists, scholars, and citizens buried him in the center of the nave of
Westminster Abbey. The black slab that
marks his resting-place bears this inscription:

Brought by faithful hands over land and sea, here
rests David Livingstone, missionary, traveler, philanthropist. For thirty years his life was spent in an
unwearied effort to evangelize the native races, to
explore the undiscovered secrets, and abolish the
desolating slave trade of Central Africa.

And there, too, are these words of his
Master's: "Other sheep I have, which are
not of this fold, them also I must bring, and
they shall hear my voice." Oh, loftiest
spirit of earth! The soul of Livingstone
surpassing those great ones who toiled for

fame and place and honors. Should it ever be our good fortune to behold those elect heroes, Paul and Savonarola and Luther and Lincoln, with all the poets and reformers and philanthropists, perhaps not far from Him whose "name is above every name" we shall see the scarred hero who lost his life to the Dark Continent indeed, but whose name glows with the brightness of the firmament and shines like the stars forever and ever.

XII

The Christian Scholar in Politics — A Study of the Life of William Ewart Gladstone

Look at the great modern statesmen who have shaped the politics of the world. They were educated men; were they, therefore, visionary, pedantic, impracticable? Cavour, whose monument is United Italy — one from the Alps to Tarentum, from the lagoons of Venice to the Gulf of Salerno; Bismarck, who has raised the German empire from a name to a fact; Gladstone, to-day the incarnate heart and conscience of England — they are the perpetual refutation of the sneer that high education weakens men for practical affairs. Trained themselves, such men know the value of training. All countries, all ages, all men, are their teachers. The broader their education, the wider the horizon of their thought and observation; the more affluent their resources, the more humane their policy. Would Samuel Adams have been a truer popular leader had he been less an educated man? Would Walpole the less truly have served his country had he been, with all his capacities, a man whom England could have revered and loved? Could Gladstone so sway England with his fervent eloquence, as the moon the tides, were he a gambling, swearing, boozing squire like Walpole? There is no sophistry more poisonous to the State, no folly more stupendous and demoralizing, than the notion that the purest character and the highest education are incompatible with the most commanding mastery of men and the most efficient administration of affairs.—*Orations and Addresses (George William Curtis), Vol. I, pp. 271, 272.*

XII

THE CHRISTIAN SCHOLAR IN POLITICS—A STUDY OF THE LIFE OF WILLIAM EWART GLADSTONE

The year 1809 was a memorable year for America and England. It saw the birth of Abraham Lincoln, the greatest of emancipators; of Charles Darwin, the greatest scientist since Isaac Newton; of William Ewart Gladstone, the greatest statesman of the Victorian era. When Edmund Burke died in 1797 Canning wrote: "There is but one event, but it is an event of the world: Burke is dead." And now that Gladstone hath passed from the strife of politics to where beyond these voices there is rest and peace, England and America have but one heart: that heart is very sore. For this man, who reverenced his conscience as his king, was also one whose "glory was redressing human wrong." At once the child of genius, wealth, and power, this young pa-

*Gladstone, The Man and His Work, by Frank W. Gunsaulus, Life of Gladstone, by Justin McCarthy.

trician took as his clients, not the rich and great, but the poor and weak. Oft through voice and pen did he plead the cause of the oppressed in Italy and Ireland, in Bulgaria and Armenia. Countless reformers and philanthropists there are in this and foreign lands who in hours of discouragement comforted themselves with the thought that this knight-errant of the poor was in Hawarden, and felt that our world was a little safer because the "great commoner" was there.

"Death bringeth good fame," said Bacon; but his splendid talents, his pure purpose and blameless deeds, brought Mr. Gladstone good fame in a life that was singularly happy and glorious. Refusing the offer of a title and a seat in the House of Lords, he chose to live and die as plain Mr. Gladstone. "Posterity," wrote Macaulay, "has obstinately refused to degrade Francis Bacon into Viscount St. Albans." And if Mr. Gladstone had no rank as earl or duke, he stood forth regal with a royalty beyond that of kings. Recently England celebrated the diamond jubilee of Queen Victoria, but in that stately and brilliant pageant Mr. Gladstone was a figure clothed

with a fascination beyond that of the greatest of England's queens. Even those who
were his political opponents affirm that
whatever is high-minded, pure, and disinterested in patriots must henceforth be
identified with his immortal tradition, while
whatever is base, selfish, or sinister in
national policy is rebuked by the lustre of
his life.

Standing upon the summit of the Alpine
mountain, the traveler looks into sunny
Italy or the German forests, toward the
vineyards of France or the far-off plains
of Austria. And Mr. Gladstone stands forth
like some sun-crowned mountain-peak, su-
premely great in every side of his character and career. He was a scholar, and
with Homer lingered long before the gates
of Troy, or with Pericles and Plato saun-
tered through the groves of Athens. He
was an author, and the mere titles of his
speeches and books fill twenty pages in the
catalogue of libraries. He was an orator,
and his eloquence was such that oft it
seemed to his rapt listeners as if Apollo
had come again—the music of the morning
breathing from his lips. He was a states-

man, and the reforms he proposed and the laws he created are milestones measuring the progress of the English people. Above all, he was a Christian gentleman, for religion goes with the name of Gladstone as poetry with the name of Burns or Browning, as war with Wellington or Washington.

Going away, he has left behind men of acute intellect, brave heart, and eloquent tongue. But having praised the statesmen who remain, let us confess that there has been but one who could first conquer and then reconcile; but one who could oppose the policy and principles for which he once stood and still retain the confidence of those whom he had come to antagonize. Like Cromwell, he had a heart of oak and hand of iron; he had the ardor and the integrity of Hampden; he had the eloquence and chivalry of Vane; like Lord Lawrence, he "feared man so little because he feared God so much"; like Washington, he had sanity and moderation. In stormy epochs it might have been said of him, "All the world was shaken, but not the intellect of Gladstone." Remembering his

character and career, England feels that
Westminster Abbey alone is worthy to con-
tain his remains. United in sorrow, the
statesmen who followed and those who
opposed Gladstone clasped hands and bore
his sacred dust into the "temple of silence
and reconciliation," where the enmities of
twenty centuries lie buried.

In his fascinating studies of Homer and
the Trojan era, Mr. Gladstone dwells upon
the character of Jupiter and Minerva, oft
descending into the tents of warriors to heal
their strifes and bickerings, to encourage
the defeated hosts, and lead them on to victory. As we watch these divine beings
leaving the Olympian heights to enter the
earthly scene, one thinks instinctively of
Gladstone himself, towering shoulders high
above all his fellows, his great, beautiful
head telling us that he, too, is of "Olympus
and Olympian." Beside other great statesmen of his century he stands forth clothed
with power and majesty as with a garment.

If we call the roll of the great orators and
advocates with whom he was associated for
five and sixty years, long is the list and
splendid the names. When Gladstone en-

tered Parliament Sir Robert Peel was there, his thoughts logic, his atmosphere grace and strength, his speech aglow with wit and humor, his presence dignity, his voice honey. O'Connell was there, with genius to awe the multitude, with pathos to melt the coldest statesman, whom Wendell Phillips called "God's anointed king, whose single word melts all wills into his." Beside O'Connell, with his passion for philanthropy, stood Brougham, a square of rough-hewn granite, conquering men by sheer weight of mentality, great as advocate, agitator, and orator. Nor must Palmerston be forgotten, the proud and stately statesman, distinguished as foreign secretary, who had taken the affairs of all foreign nations as his department, as Bacon once took "all knowledge as his province." There, too, was Macaulay the essayist, and Grote the historian, and Bulwer the novelist, and Cobden the friend of the common people, the corn-law agitator, whose power was sincerity, whose character exhaled sweetness and simplicity, whose influence, once the "corn laws" were repealed, was for a time well-nigh supreme.

Another close friend of Mr. Gladstone was John Bright, the Quaker orator, who had modeled his speech upon the simple Saxon of the Bible and John Bunyan, a man of superb physique and marvelous voice, with a certain gift of humor and an eloquence that, while restrained, yet burned at white heat; Disraeli, whose pastime was novel-writing, whose idol was politics, with a will of iron and conscience of india-rubber, with a genius for sarcasm, who could open the gates of speech and pour forth a flood of vitriolic acid. In later years, also, Mr. Gladstone had his opponents. Among these was Lord Randolph Churchill, with his passion for invective, from whom England hoped so much, but who for want of moral purpose achieved so little; Mr. Balfour, the metaphysician, boasting that he never read a newspaper, writing on psychological problems, whose "light reading before breakfast is Plato and Aristotle," the most charming of opponents, with an easy, contemptuous smile at the moment when he sheathes his sword in the bowels of his opponent. Another rival was Lord Salisbury, who, with all the responsibility of the prime ministry, has found time to be president of the British Society for the Advancement of Scientific Research, an original investigator in the problems of electricity, whose arguments for theism from the viewpoint of science have been so highly praised —a statesman admired for his comprehensive knowledge, solidity, and cautious judgment, a man who has made all England to be his debtor. When we call the roll of the great men with whom Gladstone was associated, we see that this has been indeed an age of giants. Mr. Gladstone had his faults, and made mistakes that were not few, but in amplitude of faculty, fertility of resource, in the richness and variety of his gifts and achievements, he stands forth easily the first statesman of the Victorian era.

Renowned as orator and author, as philanthropist and Christian reformer, his ancestry accounts only in a degree for Mr. Gladstone's greatness. For the most part the hidings of his power are wrapt in clouds and mystery. Through a long line of noble forefathers, nature and providence began to make ready for the giant two hun-

It was a Scotsman who went to Lombard
Street and founded the Bank of England.
It was a Scotsman who went to the Avenue
in Paris and founded the Bank of France.
And Mr. Gladstone came naturally by his
genius for finance, that made his fame as
chancellor of the exchequer. In his study
of Jennie Deans, Scott makes her tell the
truth, even though it threatens her sister's
life. And Gladstone also hated every form
of lying, and was frank to the point of
rudest bluntness. Every Scotsman cher-
ishes the secret belief that he knows all
about God. And true to the national characteristic, Mr. Gladstone explored the
nooks and corners of every known theological system. The Scotsman also believes in
education, and so when the child was thir-
teen years of age he appeared at Eton—
"the handsomest boy," said the famous
naturalist Murchison, "that ever entered the
historical school," as later on men said that
Gladstone was "the handsomest old man
who ever appeared in Parliament," age never
having dimmed the fire of his eyes.

To all his other gifts nature added a
genius for friendship. In Eton College his

dearest friend was Arthur Hallam, whose gifts, virtues, and untimely death Tennyson laments in the noblest poem of this century, "In Memoriam." Among his close friends at Eton and Oxford were Tennyson, Canning, Maurice, Lowe, and that youth who was to be known as Cardinal Manning. "No man," said Bishop Wordsworth, "ever heard Gladstone speak in his student days at Oxford who did not feel that he would rise to be prime minister of England." An indomitable physical constitution, a powerful reason, a perfect memory, an intuitive knowledge of men, rare common sense, imagination, moral enthusiasm, sincerity, earnestness, wealth, social position — all these stars glow in the constellation of his genius. Nature and providence denied no talent that could aid him in achieving a great career.

Reviewing this illustrious life, we see that the genius of Gladstone's life was the genius of patriotism. The child of leisure, relinquishing long-cherished plans for the pulpit through the pressure of his father's iron will, he determined to enter Parliament, and bring to the questions of practical legislation the patient study, the wide research, the trained faculties that Isaac Newton brought to his work in astronomy, and Bacon to his work in philosophy, and Gibbon to his work in history. Believing in the leadership of educated men, he outlined his career as that of a scholar in politics. He felt that every sneer at the scholar is the sneer of the demagogue, plotting some form of treason against the state. He knew that the foundations of law and jurisprudence go back to a scholar named Moses. He knew that the golden age of Athens was ushered in by a scholar named Pericles. He knew that Florence and Venice and Oxford and London had their foundations in wisdom and knowledge; and that from the day "when Themistocles led the educated Athenians at Salamis to that when Von Moltke marshaled the educated Germans against France, the foundations of states are not laid in ignorance." Emulating the Puritan poet Milton, Gladstone the student seems to have looked forward to the time when he might enter the arena of Parliament to attack selfish rulers, class privileges, and ancient abuses. Certainly, had he foreseen the day when he should stand forth in deadly conflict with leaders of wrong against humanity, he could scarcely have prepared himself more carefully.

Leaving the lecture-halls and libraries at Oxford, the eager youth remembered that he lived in an historic land, hallowed by the life and death of patriots, poets, heroes. A pilgrim to England's sacred shrines, one day he turned his steps toward Runnymede, where brave barons wrested "the great charter" from an ignoble king. He made his way to Hampton Court, and mused upon Wolsey's vast ambition. He turned his steps toward the House of Parliament, and in imagination heard Burke close his immortal speech against Hastings. He sought out John Milton's tomb, and read again the scholar's plea for the freedom of the press. He entered the great abbey, and standing beside the memorials of England's greatest statesmen, he recalled famous men of old — kings, counselors, patriots prodigal of their blood, just men by whom impartial laws were given; and standing there, the genius of the abbey whispered to him that only the ripest training, the purest

moment that it disappears in the vast ocean that lies beyond.

As a scholar and author his crowning characteristic was his intellectual hospitality. At eighty years of age, mentally he was still growing with the rapidity of a boy. His rule was to take up at least one new subject every three months. Therefore his life increased in freshness and zest as it advanced in years. For him life's best wine was reserved for the last of the feast. The most fascinating period of Gladstone's career was between the years named—seventy and eighty-five. With biting sarcasm Disraeli once taunted him with being inconsistent, affirming that no man knew to-day what Gladstone would think or say to-morrow. He began, indeed, as a Tory, but ended as a Radical. During his long career his political views passed through many changes, but these changes represent, not fickleness, but the evolution of a scholar. His growth was first the blade, then the ear, then the full corn in the ear. One of the tests of greatness is growth. Mediocrity is never mistaken. The two-talent man cannot afford to confess that he was wrong yes-

terday. But genius, conscious of infinite
reserves, can afford to confess its mistakes.
Now and then a politician declares that he
believes to-day just what he believed ten
years ago, and has made no change, serenely
unconscious of the fact that this is equiva-
lent to the fact that he has not had an idea
in ten years. He who believes to-day what
he believed a year ago may as well order his
burial robes—his place is in the cemetery.
Mr. Gladstone was alive and eager, and his
growth registered itself in changes. Providence marched on, and the statesman
marched on with Him. In his youth Gladstone was a pioneer, and in extreme old age
he was still a scout, opening up new paths
in the wilderness. He was an optimist, an
innovator, and through all the smoke of
battle and defeat he saw afar off the final
victory.

Reviewing his political career, Lord Salisbury has said that Mr. Gladstone will be
remembered less for his political achievements than for his Christian ideals in politics. His whole career was devoted to the
attempt to reconcile politics to the Sermon
on the Mount, just as John Stuart Mill tried

to reconcile politics with political economy. Therefore the reforms that Gladstone proposed, the principles he advocated, register his attempt to carry political legislation up to the level of ideal morals. In his first book on church and state he lifted up an ideal standard, and boldly asserted that the state must have a conscience, and having a conscience, will be the better for taxing itself for the support of a state religion. Then came the free-trade struggle, in which he threw himself against the landed interests of his family and his class, joining Cobden and Bright in a movement to open the ports of England to the grain markets of the world. Having heard of the sufferings of political prisoners in Naples, he determined to give up his holiday and investigate the question. He found means to visit the prisons, and saw these patriots in their dungeons. Having searched the question to the bottom, he addressed a letter to the whole civilized and Christian world, in which he denounced this treatment of political prisoners as a blot upon civilization, religion, humanity, and decency. He affirmed that the rule of Ferdinand was the negation of God erected into a government. Through these letters he won from the Italians the credit of being "one of the founders of free Italy."

Then came his repeal of the taxes upon education, his movement for popular suffrage, the disestablishment of the Irish church, the movement for national education, his plea for Bulgaria, for home rule in Ireland, for the universality of the tenant-right custom, and last of all he lifted his shield above the oppressed in Armenia and Crete. Against his own landed and hereditary interests he made himself the client of the poor and lowly. He was disinterested, and had a magnificent disregard of popularity, and therefore proudly independent. He achieved the distinction of being one of the most cordially hated men of his era. With the simple ingenuousness of a child, he believed that ideal Christianity is the only practical politics. Therefore, where he began his career there he ended it, affirming that England could lead the grand procession of the nations only as she herself walked in the paths of religion and peace that Jesus Christ had opened.

The Christian Scholar in Politics

But that for which Mr. Gladstone will be chiefly remembered is his characteristic as a Christian scholar in politics. What color is to Raphael, what music is to Mozart, what philosophy is to Bacon, that religion was to Gladstone. His earliest passion and his latest enthusiasm was the passion and enthusiasm for the character and teachings of Jesus Christ. An indefatigable student of Homer, Dante, and Shakespeare, the literature of which he was most fond was the Bible. As the knights of the Round Table served King Arthur, so, but far more faithfully, he sought to serve our "Great Master, Christ." Statesman and financier, he was also seer and disciple. No Puritan was ever more severe in his emphasis of method and habit in his Christian life. So scrupulous was he in his recognition of the Sabbath day, that, though four times prime minister, he absolutely refused to receive upon the Sabbath one of the government officials, or to discuss any political crisis or measure. Going into the pulpit on Sunday to read prayers in the church of Hawarden, each morning of the six week days he also made his way to the same little church to bow

while the rector read daily prayers. When
prime minister for the last time he brought
an old coachman up to London for medical
treatment, and having found suitable quar-
ters, he charged his physician to send him
word should a crisis come. The end came
at an hour when Mr. Gladstone was in an
important discussion with Sir William Har-
court. In that hour the prime minister
dropped everything, and hurrying to another part of the city, he lent his old servant
comfort as he passed down into the dark
valley, and this servant died while the prime
minister of England was praying to the
Eternal God, who is Lord of death and life
alike, just as, while his own son read the
solemn prayer, he himself passed on into
realms of happiness and immortal peace.

Great as Gladstone was as orator, scholar,
and statesman, he was greater still as a
Christian. With all the enthusiasm of a
young soldier for some noble general, of
a pupil for some artist master, he poured
forth all his gifts and ambitions at the be-
hest of his divine Master and Saviour.

Gladstone belonged to a race of giants,
not only because he was great in himself,

but also because long companionship lent him something of the majesty of his divine Master. For the secret of the success of this hero who was at once orator, scholar, and statesman, is the secret of the Messiah.

Noisy to-day are the skeptics, but should we mention the name of some one of these doubters best known for talent, and multiply his work a thousand-fold, yet, set over against the sublime achievements and the massive character of Gladstone, he would seem as a mud hut over against a marble house. The lesson of this great life is that the most splendid gifts, opportunities, and ambitions should be given to Him who said, "Inasmuch as ye have done it unto one of the least of these my brethren ye have done it unto Me."

INDEX

Index

Index

335

Index

Index

Index

Index

Printed in the United States of America.